Landscapes of
FUERTEVENTURA

a countryside guide
Sixth edition

Noel Rochford

Sixth edition © 2015
Sunflower Books™
PO Box 36160
London SW7 3WS, UK
www.sunflov

ISBN 978-1-85691-459-8

Betancuria (Car tour 1, Walk 9)

Important note to the reader

We have tried to ensure that the descriptions and maps in this book are error-free at press date. The book will be updated, where necessary, whenever future printings permit. It will be very helpful for us to receive your comments (sent in care of the publishers, please) for the updating of future printings.

We also rely on those who use this book — especially walkers — to take along a good supply of common sense when they explore. Conditions change fairly rapidly on Fuerteventura, and *storm damage or bulldozing may make a route unsafe at any time*. If the route is not as we outline it here, and your way ahead is not secure, return to the point of departure. *Never attempt to complete a tour or walk under hazardous conditions!* Please read carefully the Country code on page 15 and the notes on pages 33 to 37, as well as the introductory comments at the beginning of each tour and walk (regarding road conditions, equipment, grade, distances and time, etc). Explore *safely*, while at the same time respecting the beauty of the countryside.

Cover: Playa de Sotavento de Jandía — queen of Fuerteventura's beaches
Title page: windmill at Valles de Ortega

Sunflower Books and 'Landscapes' are Registered Trademarks.
Photographs pages 1, 2, 12, 15, 20 (top), 21, 23, 30-1, 32, 51 (bottom), 56-7, 61 (top), 67, 70 (top), 71, 82 (top), 108-9, 111, 112 (all), 114-5, 116-7, 120-1, 125 (bottom): John Underwood; 19, 20 (bottom), 22, 34-5, 38, 39, 41, 48, 51 (top), 52, 53, 66, 74 (top), 79 (bottom), 86-7, 90-1, 100 (all), 101 (bottom): Conny Spelbrink; all others: the author
Maps and plans: Sunflower Books; walking maps Datum WGS84, UTM (28R) projection with 1km grid squares
A CIP catalogue record for this book is available from the British Library.
Printed and bound in England: Short Run Press, Exeter

Contents

4   Landscapes of Fuerteventura

Landscape near Betancuria

🌻 Preface

Fuerteventura is different from all the other islands in the Canaries. Being the closest to Africa, there's a definite taste of the Sahara about it. The landscape is thirsty, barren and severe.

In two things this island excels and outdoes all the others in the archipelago: it has the best beaches and the best climate. Beaches are what Fuerteventura is all about — mile upon mile of untouched golden sand, great billowing white sand dunes, foaming surf, and quiet turquoise coves. If you're after sea and sun, this is the island for you! Windsurfers, too, have discovered the perfect winds to enjoy their hobby.

Although the scenery changes little, it's pleasant to tour Fuerteventura's timeless landscapes by car. The island's beauty spots are tucked away, often out of sight. I hope this book will help you find them. But please — if you are hiring a jeep or a bike, keep to the main tracks and do not travel cross-country: Fuerteventura's dunes are home to very rare birds, some of which lay their well-camouflaged eggs directly on the ground. To protect these birds, some parts of the island are under state protection — for instance, the dunes of Corralejo.

In case you get tired of the beaches (which is fairly unlikely), or there's an overcast, cool day, there is quite a bit of walking to be enjoyed on Fuerteventura. You needn't be an inveterate hiker: there are walks to suit all appetites — rambles across the old worn hills, fairly easy mountain ascents, seaside hikes and, for explorers, rocky *barrancos* in which to flounder. Even the picnic spots will help you get better acquainted with the island. There are hidden streams, palm groves, and crystal-clear lagoons just waiting to be discovered. Lobos — the tiny island of 'anthills' — is another world again. It's a charmer.

Fuerteventura is the richest of the islands in Guanche relics (sorry, Gran Canaria). Few people are aware of this. The island is littered with Guanche settlements — all untouched. Unfortunately, they are also mostly unprotected and crumbling away. Admittedly, most are hard to distinguish or are well off the beaten track; hence I've only mentioned a couple of these sites in the book.

Tourism, after having side-stepped this island for many

years, struck suddenly like a bolt of lightning, leaving the populace reeling from the blow. Being reserved in character by nature, they were very wary of it all. So at first you may not find all the Fuerteventurans as openly friendly as other Canarians. Speaking some Spanish can make a big difference, especially amongst the village folk and those not involved in tourism.

Landscapes of Fuerteventura will, I hope, give you a better insight into this now-booming tourist mecca.

Acknowledgements

I would like to express my thanks to the staff of the Patronato de Turismo and the island Cabildo, for all their help when I was preparing the original edition of this book. For later editions, my special thanks to Conny Spelbrink and to my publishers, Sunflower Books, who between them periodically check and revise all the tours and walks when I'm not able to revisit the Canaries.

Further reading

Titles in the 'Landscapes' series are countryside guides, intended for use in tandem with a general guide — of which there are many available. Two reference books which I particularly treasure are *Wild Flowers of the Canary Islands* by David and Zoë Bramwell and *Crafts and Traditions of the Canary Islands* by Michael Eddy. Both are out of print at time of writing, but available on the web from various suppliers (at hefty prices, so try your local library first!).

If you enjoy using this book, I've written several other 'Landscapes' for the Canaries: *Tenerife (Orotava • Anaga • Teno • Cañadas); La Gomera and Southern Tenerife; La Palma and El Hierro; Lanzarote; Gran Canaria* (all published by Sunflower Books).

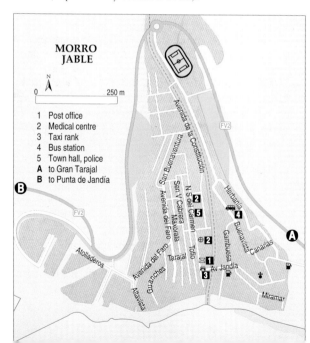

MORRO JABLE

0   250 m

1 Post office
2 Medical centre
3 Taxi rank
4 Bus station
5 Town hall, police
A to Gran Tarajal
B to Punta de Jandía

❀ Getting about

On Fuerteventura it's a good idea to hire a vehicle for at least part of your holiday. **Car hire** on the island is very reasonable, with all hire firms offering competitive rates.

Taxis fares are not particularly high, but you *do* have to travel long distances to get anywhere. Sharing the taxi with others lessens the blow. Taxis use meters for all journeys, even long distance drives, so make sure that the meter is turned on! At all the major resorts you will find a list of prices to the most common destinations — usually at the taxi stand. If you want to know approximately how much your journey will cost, you can compare distances with one of the more popular routes before you set off.

Coach tours are easy to arrange and get you to all the tourist points of interest, but never off the beaten track.

The **local bus** service has improved dramatically in recent years. There is good service between the resorts themselves and to/from Puerto del Rosario. But buses to inland villages are still severely limited (often just one a day), so you may need private transport to reach any hikes in these outposts. Selected bus timetables are shown on page 126, but you are likely to find more convenient lines operating from your resort once you are on the island.

Don't rely *solely* on our timetables. Re-check the timetables at www.tiadhe.com, where you'll also find information about bus fares. If you plan to use the buses often, be sure to invest in a 'bono' card, which offers a **30%** discount on all fares (and can also be shared with other users). Finally: although some buses may run late, I'd advise you *always to arrive about 15 minutes*

1 Tourist information	5 Post office
2 Police	6 Bus stop
3 Market	7 Medical centre
4 Restaurante Frasquita	8 Shopping centre
	9 Los Geranios

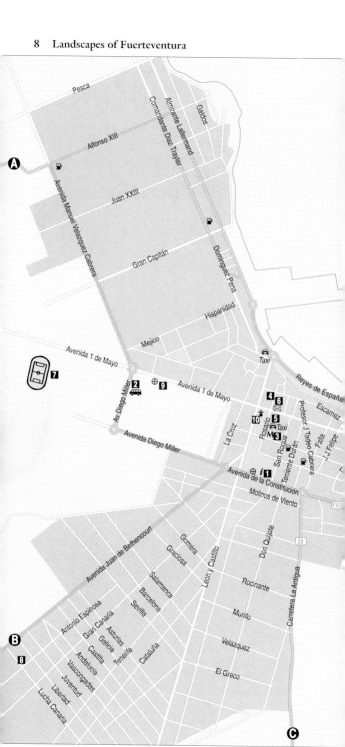

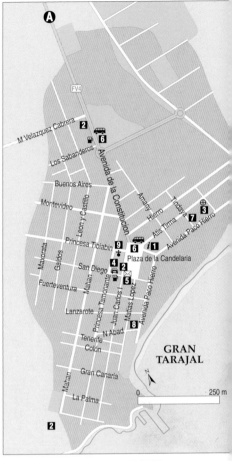

PUERTO DEL ROSARIO

GRAN TARAJAL

PUERTO DEL ROSARIO
1 Tourist information
2 Bus station
3 Casa Museo de
   Unamuno
4 Town hall and police
5 Island council
   (Cabildo)
6 Post office
7 Sports ground
8 (near Exit B) Medio
   Ambiente offices
9 Medical centre
10 Nuestra Señora del
   Rosario
A to Corralejo
B to La Oliva
C to Casillas del Angel
D to hospital and airport

GRAN TARAJAL
1 Tourist information
2 Telephones
3 Medical centre
4 Taxi rank
5 Post office
6 Bus stop
7 Police
8 Market
9 San Diego
A to Tuineje

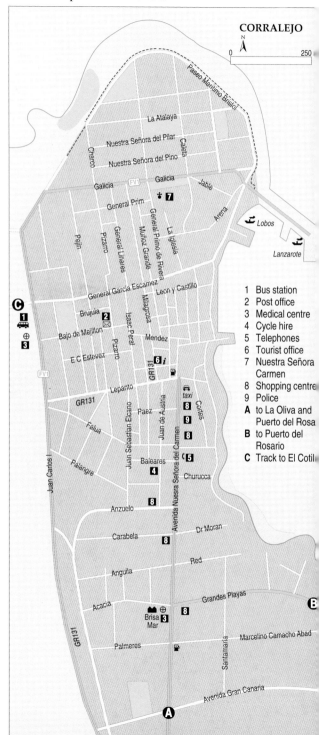

CORRALEJO

1 Bus station
2 Post office
3 Medical centre
4 Cycle hire
5 Telephones
6 Tourist office
7 Nuestra Señora Carmen
8 Shopping centre
9 Police
A to La Oliva and Puerto del Rosa
B to Puerto del Rosario
C Track to El Cotil

☀ Picnicking

Most tourists come here for the beaches and the sunshine. There are enough beautiful beaches on this island to visit a different one each day for a month. Many of them are off the beaten track, and this means taking along a picnic hamper if you intend to spend the day there. And it's a good idea to carry a large umbrella because there is generally little or *no* shade.

Finding other picnic spots, however, is a different story. There are no 'organised' picnic places on Fuerteventura, unlike on some of the other Canary Islands. The picnic settings I've suggested are therefore natural beauty spots I've discovered on my walks. My own personal favourite is Lobos … when it's not too windy!

On the following pages you'll find my suggestions for some lovely picnic spots, together with all the information you need to reach them. *Note that picnic numbers correspond to walk numbers;* thus you can quickly find the general location on the island by referring to the pull-out touring map (where the walks are outlined in green). Most of the spots I've chosen are very easy to reach, and I include transport details (🚌/⛴: bus or ferry information; 🚗: where to park if travelling by car), walking times, and views or setting. Beside the picnic title, you'll also find page references for maps and photographs. The *precise* location of the picnic spot is shown on the relevant large-scale *walking* map by the symbol *P*, printed in green. All of the picnics are also illustrated, to whet your appetite.

Please glance over the comments before you start off on your picnic: if some walking is involved, remember to wear sensible shoes and to take a sunhat (○ = picnic in full sun). It's a good idea to take along a plastic sheet as well, in case the ground is damp.

If you are travelling to your picnic by car, be extra vigilant off the main roads and *never* block a road or track when you park. While I've recommended a car for getting to and from almost all these picnic spots, in fact many are accessible by bus as well — you'll just have a somewhat longer walk. (These picnic suggestions make ideal short walks however you are getting about on the island.)

All picnickers should read the country code on page 15 and go quietly in the countryside. *Buen provecho!*

1 LOBOS (map page 40, photographs pages 38-39, 41) ○

🚶: 10-15min on foot. Ferry from Corralejo to/from Lobos.
Head left as you leave the jetty; less than 10min along, you'll spot a path branching off left, into the sand dunes. This leads to lovely Playa de la Concha. If you prefer swimming off rocks, try the stunning setting of Casas El Puertito just 5min from the jetty — *to the right*. Both are superb, tranquil spots.

2 FARO DE TOSTON (map pages 46-47, photographs pages 42-43, 48) ○

🚌 to/from the Faro de Tostón: 5-10min on foot. Park at the side of the road to the lighthouse, north of El Cotillo.
Picnic at any of the delightful turquoise coves or on the dunes near the lighthouse.

5 LA OLIVA (map pages 58-59, photographs pages 55, 56-57)

🚌 (Lines: 07, 08): 10-15min on foot. From the bus stop, walk to the Casa de los Coroneles, signposted from the church.
🚌: 5min on foot. Park in the car park in front of the Casa de los Coroneles in La Oliva.
Follow Walk 5 (page 55) to reach the ruined homestead directly behind the Casa de los Coroneles. This is a pleasant spot from where you can admire the Casa de los Coroneles without the tourists, or look out east to the impressive Montaña del Frontón. Some shade from a few palms or the walls of this derelict, but charming homestead.

9 BETANCURIA (map pages 70-71, photographs pages 2, 69, 70)

🚌 or 🚌 (Line 02) to/from Betancuria: 15-20min on foot, with a steady climb of up to 100m/330ft.
Follow Alternative walk 9 (page 68) out of Betancuria and picnic anywhere on the grassy slopes above the last houses ... out of sight of the dogs, or you'll get no peace! There is a good outlook over the village. There is no shade until you get up into the stubby pines.

Landscape at the Presa de las Peñitas (near Picnic 10)

10 BARRANCO DE LAS PEÑITAS (map pages 72-73, photographs pages 74-75 and below) ○

🚗: 10-20min on foot. Park by the bridge on the Presa de las Peñitas road, as described in 'How to get there' on page 72.
Follow Walk 10 on page 73 to reach the dam wall and descend *with care* to the chapel (Nuestra Señora de la Peña), which offers the only shade in this sun-baked setting.

11a BARRANCO DE LA MADRE DEL AGUA (map pages 72-73, photograph page 76-77)

🚗: 7-10min on foot. Park at the *barranco* bed, near Ajuy. To get there, take the Ajuy road out of Pájara, and after 9km turn off onto a track, just past a lone house (on a bend in the road, just *before* you come into Ajuy). Park in the *barranco* bed or, if you have a four-wheel drive vehicle, you can drive up to the picnic spot.
Head up the bed of the *barranco* for 7min, until you reach a narrow valley choked with palms. A little way in, you'll find it has a lovely little brook with a footbridge. Picnicking in a setting like this is rare indeed on Fuerteventura!

11b CALETA NEGRA (map pages 72-73, photograph page 78) ○

🚗: 15-20min on foot. Park at the turning circle at the entrance to Ajuy, in the village itself, or directly on the beach.
Follow the path on the right-hand side of the beach uphill — in other words, just follow the rest of the crowd. Then use the notes for Walk 11 on page 77 to reach the gate not far above the *mirador,* from where you can continue around the bay — not too close to the cliff-edge! — in welcome solitude. No shade.

12 PUERTO DE LA TORRE (map page 81, photograph page 82)

🚗: 5 min on foot. Park at Puerto de la Torre: the turn off is 3km south of Caleta de Fuste, on the FV2. Drive into Las Salinas, then continue south, first along the road and then along a short stretch of track, to Puerto de la Torre.
The best place to picnic is in the thin grove of palms which offers plenty of shade, five minutes back off the beach.

13 GINIGINAMAR (map page 85, photograph page 84) ○

🚗: 10-15min on foot, with a steep gravelly climb at the start. Park in Giniginamar.
Walk to the right-hand (western) end of the beach and climb the gravelly path up the hillside behind the houses. You'll have a good view over this quiet little fishing village, and along the coastline. No shade.

17 PLAYA DE COFETE (map pages 96-97, photograph page 101) ○

🚗 *(jeep or 4-wheel drive only):* up to 5min on foot. Take the first turn-off left outside Cofete hamlet to the beaches of Cofete and Barlovento de Jandía. Park on the beach.
Picnic anywhere. Note that the sea is very dangerous; treat it with respect. No shade.

☀ Touring

Most visitors to Fuerteventura hire a vehicle for all or part of their stay. Car hire is not expensive. Do shop around, while at the same time bearing in mind that cheapest is not always best! Always check your vehicle in advance and point out any existing dents, scratches, etc. Ask for all the conditions and insurance cover in writing, in English. Check to make sure you have a sound spare tyre and all the necessary tools. Be sure to get the office *and the after-hours* telephone numbers of the car hire firm and carry them with you. If you're not 100% happy about the car, don't take it. Finally, if you pay by credit card, make a note of exactly what you're signing for. *Important:* Leave nothing of value in your car, and always lock it. Car theft is not unknown.

The touring notes are brief: they contain little history or information readily available in free tourist office leaflets or standard guide books. The main tourist centres and towns are not described either, for the same reason. Instead, I concentrate on the 'logistics' of touring: times and distances, road conditions, and seeing places many tourists miss. Most of all I emphasise possibilities for **walking** and **picnicking**. While some of the references to walks and picnics off the beaten track may not be suitable during a long car tour, you may see a landscape that you would like to explore at leisure another day, when you've more time to stretch your legs.

The large fold-out touring map is designed to be held out opposite the touring notes and contains all the information you will need outside the towns. **Town plans**, showing exits for motorists, are on pages 6-10. The two largest resorts on the island are Corralejo and Morro Jable, so I have based the drives around these two centres. The best car tour, in my opinion, is Tour 1 — with the Jandía Peninsula tacked on to it.

Remember to allow plenty of time for visits, and to take along warm clothing as well as some food and drink, in case you are delayed. The distances in the touring notes are *cumulative* from the departure point. A key to the **symbols** in the touring notes is on the touring map.

All motorists should read the country code on page 15 and go quietly in the countryside. *Buen viaje!*

A country code for walkers and motorists

The experienced rambler is used to following a country code, but the tourist out for a lark may unwittingly cause damage, harm animals, or even endanger his own life. Please heed this advice.

- **Do not light fires.**
- **Do not frighten animals.**
- The **dunes** in the north as well as in the south are the home of very rare birds, some of which lay their well-camouflaged eggs directly on the ground. They could easily be destroyed by jeeps or mountain bikes, so please *keep to the main tracks and do not travel cross-country.*
- **Walk quietly** through all hamlets and villages.
- **Leave all gates just as you find them.**
- **Protect all wild and cultivated plants.** Don't try to pick wild flowers or uproot saplings. Obviously fruit and other crops are someone's private property and should not be touched. Never walk over cultivated land.
- **Take all your litter away with you.**
- **Walkers — *Do not take risks!*** This is the most important point of all. Do not attempt walks beyond your capacity, and do not wander off the paths described here if there is any sign of mist or if it is late in the day. Never walk alone (four is the best walking group), and always tell a responsible person exactly where you are going and what time you plan to return. Remember, if you become lost or injure yourself, it may be a long time before you are found. On any but a short walk close to villages, be sure to take a compass, whistle, torch, extra water and warm clothing — as well as some high-energy food, like chocolate. Read and re-read the important note on page 2, as well as guidelines on grade and equipment for each walk you plan to do!

Little 'tents' of cane are often seen dotting the countryside.

Car tour 1: THE BEST OF FUERTEVENTURA

Morro Jable • La Pared • Pájara • Betancuria • Antigua • Gran Tarajal • Las Playitas • Morro Jable

190km/118mi; 5 hours' driving; Exit A from Morro Jable

En route: Picnics 9, 10, 11a-b, 13 (see pages 12-13 and *P* symbol in the text); Walks 8, 9, 10, 11, 13, 14, 15, 16, 18

The main north-south road (FV2) is generally good. Inland roads are good, but narrow. Between Pájara and Vega de Río Palmas the road is quite high and winding. Watch out for animals on the roads in the countryside, and for pedestrians in the villages. Local people seem to drive very fast, so stay alert. Note also that it can be very windy.

Opening hours
Iglesia Santa María and adjacent Museo de Arte Sacro (Betancuria): 09.30-17.00 Mon-Fri; 09.30-14.00 Sat;
Casa Museo (of archaeology; Betancuria) 10.00-17.00 Tue-Sat; 11.00-14.00 Sun;
Windmill Crafts Center (Antigua) 10.00-18.00 daily;
Windmill Interpretation Center (Tiscamanita) 10.00-18.00 daily.

This drive takes you to some of the best sights on the island, from the most stunning beaches to the most picturesque valleys. You will be treated not only to the beauty spots, but also to the geographical and geological wonders of the island. And the final ingredient to flavour this tour to perfection is the little village of Betancuria — Fuerteventura's ancient former capital.

Leaving Morro Jable, take the FV2 (Exit A). Out of the eyesore of development that is quickly spreading north, you wind in and out of the deep bare *barrancos* that cleave the mountainous backbone of the Jandía Peninsula. Pick up the FV2 expressway at the Aldiana Club. Pico de la Zarza (806m/2645ft), the island's highest summit, can be seen at the end of both the Vinamar and Butihondo valleys. It's a modest peak that rises a mere shoulder above its off-siders. On a fine day, however, you can have a most enjoyable hike there (Walk 16). Leave the expressway at the sign 'Butihondo' and follow the old road (FV602).

Close on 16km out of Morro Jable, just as you leave the Barranco los Canarios (✕🍴), you round a bend and come to a stunning view (📷) over the captivating **Playa de Sotavento de Jandía★** — the queen of Fuerteventura's beaches (see photographs on the cover and page 105). A track forks to the right off the bend in the road here and descends to the beach below. Pull over onto this track, so that you can really appreciate this magnificent coastal vista or, if you want to get closer still, drive down this track (or down the road to the Hotel Gorriones, 5km further on). The beach widens into an expansive sand bar, and the sea will no doubt be dotted with a myriad of colourful windsurfs. Sotavento is also the highlight of Walk 18 — a marathon hike from Morro Jable to Costa Calma along the shore. In the background the coastline curves sharply to the right, and off the beach rise the giant sand hills of the Pared isthmus. Just before you reach Costa Calma, wind generators come into view through the hills on the left (photograph page 90). They're landmarks on Walks 14 and 15, both of which start at Costa Calma and cross the isthmus. **Costa Calma** (25km 🏨▲✕🅿) has tried to mitigate the worst effects of touristic development with pleasant landscaping.

Some 27km from Morro Jable, at a roundabout 1.5km beyond Costa Calma, turn off left for La Pared. After 5km

The Barranco de las Peñitas, one of the island's most picturesque valleys

you reach **La Pared** (32km 🏔 🍴⚓), a pretty *urbanización* with lots of greenery — an oasis in the desolate and naked landscape on the outskirts of the dunes. Continuing towards Pájara, cloud-catching hills rise on the right — Montaña Cardones (691m/2265ft) is the highest. The landscape is a mixture of sharp ridges and smooth rounded hills. You pass the quiet cultivated valley of **Huertas de Chilegua** (🍴), and the road climbs into these smooth rounded hills — ochre-coloured mounds of the the oldest hill formations on the island. Crossing a pass (📷) you have an unsurpassed view of the sea on the left and inland down a narrow valley. A sea of ridges and valleys cuts up the bleak landscape ahead. Soon after, a *'zona militar'* sign warns that you're passing a prohibited area (a firing range).

Descending to another isolated farmstead, look carefully for small earthen reservoirs in the valley floor. These are called *presas secas* (dry reservoirs), because they have been built to catch the water that comes down the *barrancos,* but they do not retain it. The water passes through the permeable soil into wells which have been sunk some 17-20m (about 60ft) below the ground in front of these *presas.* The small metal windpumps you see everywhere are used to bring this water up to ground level again (see photographs pages 4 and 70-71).

Through the hills, down on the coast, you may catch sight of a shipwreck washed ashore. If you want to see it at close quarters, take the gravel road forking off left some 8.5km down from the pass, signposted 'Playa La Solapa' and 'Garcey'. Go down all the way to the coast (Playa La Solapa) and, just before reaching the beach, turn left for Playa Garcey and the shipwreck.

Closer to Pájara the hills open out into a vast depression. Meet a junction (54km) and turn left on the FV621, to descend to Ajuy/Puerto de la Peña. Rounding a bend, you look down into a valley lush with palm trees, tamarisk shrubs and garden plots. Watch for the small ravine crammed with palms cutting back off it, into the hills running down on the right. This ravine, the Barranco de la Madre del Agua (**P**11a), boasts the only permanently-flowing stream on Fuerteventura. It's only a trickle, but the picnic spot is enchanting (photograph pages 76-77).

Ajuy (63km), a small village set on the edge of a black-sand beach (**Puerto de la Peña**), is one of two fishing settlements on the west coast. The dramatically sited ancient port here is well worth a visit, as is the Mirador

The church at Pájara, dedicated to the Virgen de la Regla, is especially noted for the much-photographed 'Aztec' stone carvings around the main entrance.

Caleta Negra (📷). This viewpoint (photograph page 78), and the port itself, lie north of the village, some 10 minutes' walk around the cliffs — just follow the crowds! The *mirador* sits in the cliff-face like a balcony, from where you look straight across to some sea-caves. You can also take steps down into two sea-caves directly below the viewpoint. But after visiting the *mirador*, I'd suggest you follow the notes for Walk 11 to get away from the crowds (**P**11b) since, fortunately, few tourists venture beyond the viewpoint. Just keep well away from the edge of the cliffs!

From Ajuy return to the junction and keep straight on to **Pájara** (74km ✝ ▲▲ ✗ and swimming pool). This is a large farming community surrounded by hills. The shady village is a welcoming sight, with its abundance of trees and small colourful gardens. Don't miss the church here; it is especially noteworthy for the striking 'Aztec' stone-carved decoration above the main entrance. Quite a curiosity because, along with a similar lot of sculptures in La Oliva, these carvings are unique in the Canary Islands. The two naves inside the church date back to 1645 and 1687, while the carving over the door is thought to date from the 1500s.

Leaving Pájara, take the road for Vega de Río Palmas (FV30); it's at the left of the church. Again you ascend into the hills, climbing a narrow winding road that hugs the sheer inclines (some people might find this stretch unnerving, although it is built up at the side). There are excellent views back over the Barranco de Pájara. The Degollada de los Granadillos (📷) is the pass that takes you over a solid spur of rock jutting out into the valley below. From here you have a superb outlook over to the enclosing rocky ridges.

Soon, descending, you come to another large parking area overlooking the **Presa de las Peñitas** (📷), a muddy reservoir lodged in the V of the Barranco de las Peñitas. The reservoir looks deeper than it is, since it has filled up with silt; in summer it's completely dry. Groves of tamarisk trees huddle around the tail of the *presa*, and that's a good spot from which to do some bird-watching.

Green gardens step the sides of the slopes, and palm trees complement the scene. Below the reservoir lies a sheer-sided rocky ravine, the ideal hiding place for the chapel dedicated to the island's patron saint, Nuestra Señora de la Peña (⚓P10; photographs pages 74-75). This impressive ravine, one of the island's beauty spots, is well worth exploring: to park for Walk 10 or Picnic 10, turn down

Church at Tuineje (top) and Las Playitas

sharp left at the first road you encounter beyond the viewpoint. (This detour is *not* included in the main touring distances and will add up to 6km to the tour.)

The main tour keeps to the FV30 from the viewpoint. Soon the rest of the valley opens up, and a string of houses stretches along it. They're set amidst a healthy sprinkling of palms and cultivated plots — a luxuriant corner (photograph page 17). You pass the sharp left turn to the Presa de las Peñitas just before the centre of **Vega de Río Palmas** (85km), where the church on the right is also dedicated to Nuestra Señora de la Peña. Now twisting your way up the valley, you're still very much buried in the hilly interior. Notice a large abandoned field of sisal on the hillsides to the left, a short distance further on. This plant was introduced from Mexico.

At the end of this valley you come to the village of **Betancuria**★ (90km ⬧▲✕M; photographs pages 2 and 69), well hidden from the marauding Berbers of earlier centuries. It's a very picturesque collection of manorial buildings, with a grand 17th-century cathedral dedicated to Santa María. The cathedral and convent here are the oldest examples of their style in the archipelago. Relics abound in historic Betancuria. A number of the old houses have doorways and arches dating back to the 15th century. Betancuria was the capital of Fuerteventura for some 400 years, up until 1835, and was also the first episcopal seat for all the Canaries. The oldest part of the village huddles around the cathedral, where many of the once-neglected buildings have been restored. History-hunters will enjoy the cathedral and the small Museo de Arte Sacro — as well as the nearby Casa Museo on the main road. Walk 9 ends in Betancuria, having followed an old pilgrims' route over the hills from Antigua. Following Alternative walk 9 for a short time would take you to a lovely grassy picnic spot overlooking the village (**P9**).

Continuing north on the FV30 out of Betancuria, everyone passes by the 15th-century Franciscan convent of San Buenaventura, the shell of which sits below the road on the right. Inside it (unseen from the road) are the beautiful cloistered arches shown overleaf. There is also a small enclosed church near the convent — the first church on the island (but much rebuilt in the 17th century). As you zigzag up out of the valley, you can either pull over at the top of the pass or turn up right to the Mirador Morrovelosa perched on a hilltop above the pass (📷✕).

From either vantage point there is a fine panorama over a vast plain to the north. Its far-distant reaches are edged by sharp abrupt hills called *cuchillos* (knives); over to the left lie *morros* (low, smooth hills). Betancuria nestles cosily in the valley floor below. Those of you familiar with the work of Lanzarote's César Manrique will find the *mirador* building itself of interest, as Manrique supervised its planning. Inside, the environmental authorities have set up an informative exhibition about Fuerteventura's protected areas and species.

Descending, you soon pass the turn-off left to Valle de Santa Inés and Llanos de la Concepción (Walk 8). Another expansive plain stretches out below you now, edged by the buildings of Antigua. Entering **Antigua** (100km ✝♠✕☐), you come to the beautifully laid-out square, with the simple but nevertheless imposing 18th-century church shown on page 70. Walk 9 starts here. Just north of Antigua (on the Puerto del Rosario road) stands **El Molino★**, a well-preserved 200-year-old windmill, once used for grinding corn. This is part of the Antigua Windmill Crafts Center (✕WC). The windmill *(molino)* is an appropriate introduction to Antigua, because this area has the highest concentration of windmills on Fuerteventura — as you will see when you head south out of Antigua.

Left: the ruins of the Convento de San Buenaventura, on the northern outskirts of Betancuria. Right: landscape near Antigua

Now following the FV20 towards Tuineje, you're out in the country again. Palms return to the scene, and a trickle of villages is seen sitting back in the plain. Threading your way through hills, you find cultivated fields sheltering along the floors of the *barrancos*. **Agua de Bueyes** (106km ✕) is the next village en route. Three dark volcanoes — La Laguna, Liria and Los Arrabales — rupture the lake of lava that spills out over the plains on the left. This area is called the *malpais* ('badlands'). A restored windmill sits at the entrance to **Tiscamanita** (109km ✕); here you'll find the Windmill Interpretation Centre. Around **Tuineje** (112km ☗) the large *fincas* of the tomato-growers are a prominent feature in a barren landscape.

You now keep on the FV20, passing through an industrial area, to your next port of call — **Gran Tarajal** (125km ♠☗✕⊕). Coming into the island's second biggest town, you look out over lean groves of palms dispersed along the valley floor. Tamarisk *(tarajal)* shrubs add to the verdure. This small port and pretty village has a small commercial centre and an attractive boulevard lining the beach. The houses step back up the steep sides of the valley and overlook the black-sand beach that curves around the mouth of the *barranco*.

Leaving Gran Tarajal, turn off right on the FV512, eventually passing an eyesore of development. Under 1km further on you come to the island's prettiest seaside village, **Las Playitas** (131km ♠✕). Built on sheer rocky

outcrops which rise out of the mouth of the *barranco*, it is still unspoilt and conceals a lovely dark-sand beach stretching out behind it. *Detour:* Curiosity-seekers may like to drive from Las Playitas to El Faro de Entallada, a fortress-like lighthouse set at the mouth of a wide bare valley, some 6km further north. A narrow tarred road on the right (*not signposted*) leads out to it, on your return from Las Playitas. Just below the lighthouse is a spectacular *mirador* with views all the away to Jandía.

Homeward bound, from Las Playitas return to the FV20 and keep right. Then go left on the FV2 for 'Morro Jable'. Winding behind great coastal valleys, some 6.5km from the Gran Tarajal junction you pass the turn-off for the small fishing village shown on page 84, Giniginamar (♙✕*P*13). If you'd like to visit it, the detour will take 8km return. Giniginamar is the starting point for Walk 13 — a very scenic coastal hike to Tarajalejo.

Tarajalejo (152km ▲▲♙✕ and ☏ 4km to the north), which somehow always strikes me as 'unfinished', occupies the end of a sweeping beach. Short walk 13 starts and ends here. Some 4km further on, you pass a turn-off left for the small tourist resort of La Lajita (♙✕). Just past this turn-off there is a small zoo, garden centre, and a camel station offering rides. The camel trains crossing the

hills on the left here as you leave the valley really do make an impressive sight.

Now climb amidst low hills, snatching views of pretty coves with not a soul about. Mounting the top of a crest (Cuesta de la Pared, 159km 📷), you have a splendid view of Jandía, encompassing the mountainous backbone with the identical twin peaks of Zarza (Walk 16) and Mocán, and the luminous blue and green ribbon of beaches that are the fame of Fuerteventura. Shortly, you rejoin the expressway for the return to **Morro Jable** (190km).

The stepped houses of Las Playitas

Morro Jable • Punta de Jandía • Cofete • Morro Jable

71km/44mi; 3-4 hours driving; Exit B from Morro Jable

En route: Picnic 17 (see page 13 and *P* symbol in the text); Walk 17

Except for a 10km stretch of narrow tarred road at the tip of the island, the rest of the drive is on an exceptionally rough gravel road — the worst part being the leg to Cofete. In the winter this drive is only recommended for 4WD vehicles, especially the Cofete stretch! If you decide to venture off in a standard hired car, read what your rental agreement says about travelling on unsurfaced roads — and remember that there are no petrol stations out here, and nobody to help if you have car problems. The route is well frequented by jeep safaris, so be alert for the local 'rally drivers' as well as inconsiderate tourists. Avoid this route after wet weather, and note also that the peninsula is usually very windy. Watch out for the wild donkeys that roam these plains. Some are so 'wild' that they stop cars in the middle of the track to beg for something to eat by sticking their heads through the window!

As bleak and unfriendly as this landscape may appear, it is far from unappealing. The wall of ancient volcanic mountains that dominates the Jandía Peninsula harbours severe but striking valleys. An air of loneliness and calm lingers over the plains. Crossing the *cumbre* from east to west you have spectacular views: the mountains become more impressive as they sweep back up into sheer cliffs, the vast beaches more alluring with their pounding surf. The east coast shelters a number of secluded coves, the west coast flourishes splendid sweeps of sand. It's not the kind of place you'd visit to spend a day on the beach: the strong winds will blow sand in your sarnies, not to mention the bumpy ride out. But what makes this tour so alluring are these very discomforts — and the isolation of the area.

Leave Morro Jable via (Exit B) and turn off right just above the port on a road signposted to Jandía and Cofete. After 1.5km this road reverts to gravel. Heading out into one of the most desolate corners of the island, you bump your way in and out of small deep *barrancos*. Nearly all of them end at pretty sandy coves, usually accessible on rough tracks. Crossing a vast open plain, you pass a fork off to the right (just beyond a water tank on the left; 3km). It heads up into a wide valley (Gran Valle) that carves a great gap out of the Jandía massif. This valley offers an alternative route to Cofete — on foot! It's an old mule track that was once the main east/west link; Walk 17 follows it. *Note:* only about 100 metres up the Gran Valle track lies a magnificent community of rare *Euphorbia handiensis* (Jandía thistle; see photograph overleaf).

Sharp rocky ridges dominate the landscape. Low salt-resistant vegetation — *cosco, aulaga,* ice plants and *Lycium*

25

intricatum are the inhabitants of this intractable terrain. Goats roam deep in the *barrancos,* and you pass the abandoned tomato plantation of **Casas de Jorós**. Towards the end of the island the plain broadens, and the *barrancos* become less significant. The mountain chain breaks up and slowly subsides into disjointed hills. At Punta de Jandía, the tip of this boot-shaped peninsula, stands the lighthouse.

Some 11.5km out of Morro Jable, you come to the turn-off right for Cofete. Keep left here, to descend to the lighthouse. Tracks branch off to coves ensconced in the low rocky shoreline running along on the left. Approaching Puertito de la Cruz, you come onto a tarred road, which continues on to the lighthouse *(faro)* 1km further on. A lone towering wind generator dwarfs **Puertito de la Cruz** (21km ✕). The place seems more like a weekend retreat than a fishing hamlet — in summer a lot of caravans take up residence here as well. The small adjoining houses of the old village sit on the edge of the plain, looking out to sea. Try the 'Caldo de Pescado' at the unpretentious Restaurante Tenderete — a local fish soup with potatoes and vegetables … delicious! **Punta de Jandía** (📷) itself is unimpressive; however, you do have a fine view back along the deeply-dissected mountains of the peninsula. Off the point lies an underwater reef called Baja del Griego ('where the Greek sank') or 'Arrecife del Griego' ('Greek's Reef'). Some 200 years ago, a Greek ship carrying

Left: Playa de Ojos. Right: Jandía thistle (Euphorbia handiensis; *top*) *and rock sorrel* (Rumex vesicarius) *sprouting up through thorny* aulaga

passengers from Fuerteventura to Gran Canaria hit it and sank, with all lives lost.

Now heading over to the western tip of the peninsula, to Punta Pesebre, return to Puertito de la Cruz and take the narrow tarred road forking left opposite the village. Please heed the sign that warns motorists not to leave the road — this is a protected area. Soon you're overlooking the striking cove of Playa de Ojos, bordered by a limpid green sea. Notice the volcanic hues emanating from the cliff walls. **Punta Pesebre** (27km 📷) is much more dramatic than Punta de Jandía on the east coast. You have a spectacular view along the west coast — and to Las Talabijas, the deep maroon volcano on your immediate right. And if the seas are calm, the crystal clear rock pools are brilliant for a cooling dip.

Return along your outgoing route back to the Cofete junction and turn left. Zigzagging up over a pass (📷 with limited parking), a magnificent vista greets you on the far side of the *cumbre* — one of the best views on the island. You look straight along the golden beaches of Cofete and Barlovento de Jandía. Together they stretch nearly the length of the peninsula. The white-crested breakers and blue-green sea light up the sombre plain and shadowy summits. In the distance rise the billowing sand dunes of the Pared isthmus.

The road, which is both narrow and rough, is carved out of the steep face of the escarpment. It was built to enable a certain Señor Winter to build his mansion out here. Further down the track, you'll spot a thriving colony of *candelabra,* a large multi-armed, cactus-like plant resembling a chandelier. The villagers once used the latex of this plant to catch fish: they put it into rock pools to stun the fish and bring them to the surface. **Cofete** (47km ✗) is a rustic outpost of stone and cement huts and a restaurant. Señor Winter, the German who owned the peninsula, forbade anyone to live here, so it never grew into a real village. His villa (see photographs page 101) is the main feature of the plain.

Pass through Cofete and bear right. After some 200 metres a track forking left leads to a never-ending beach (**P**17). *Important:* the sea here is dangerous at all times. A cross-current runs just off the shore, and a number of tourists have drowned. *Please do not swim!* The Winter residence (now owned by a Gran Canaria hotel chain) is 1.7km away, should your curiosity get the better of you.

Follow the same route back to **Morro Jable** (71km).

Corralejo • Puerto del Rosario • La Matilla • Los Molinos • Tindaya • Vallebrón • La Oliva • El Cotillo • Corralejo

130km/81mi; under 5 hours driving; Exit B from Corralejo

En route: Picnics (2), 5, (12) (see pages 12-13 and *P* symbol in the text); Walks 2, 3, 4, 5, 6, 7, (12)

Roads are generally good. Watch out for animals on the roadsides and for pedestrians in the village streets. It can be very windy along the coast. Note that there are petrol stations only in Puerto del Rosario , La Oliva and Corralejo (not all are open on Sunday and public holidays).

The circuit that this tour follows is fascinating rather than 'beautiful'. Impressive hills and volcanoes border the great interior basins of emptiness. During the second half of the tour you wind in and out of a rough sea of lava called the *malpais* — the 'badlands' — a curious sight, with its surprising amount of plant life and greenery. And, if you're bored with the sand dunes of Corralejo, then El Cotillo will prove quite a treat, with its cliff-backed beach and dazzling turquoise coves.

Leave Corralejo on the coastal road to Puerto del Rosario (Exit B; the FV1) and head out through the dunes. This stunning stretch of white shimmering sand is further enhanced by the aquamarine sea and the purply-blue hills that rise up in the background. Lobos (Walk 1) stands out clearly on the left, offshore, with its hundreds of little hillocks and guardian volcano. Although the dunes are supposedly a natural park, a couple of hotels interrupt this unique stretch of beauty (4.5km ▲▲ ✕).

Out of this mini-desert, you cross a featureless stone-littered plain and pass a tired-looking inland urbanization — Parque Holandés (▲✕). **Puerto del Rosario** (30km ▲▲▲✕ 🛉 🚑 ⊕ M) has grown into a smallish commercial town with some nice shops and bars. (You *could* bypass it on the FV3 ring road, picking up the FV10 for Tetir at the roundabout.)

Beyond Puerto del Rosario, the tour really begins, as you head back northwest via the inland route*. Leave

---

*An alternative route back to Corralejo lies further south and would take you via Caleta de Fuste (▲▲▲✕*P*12; Walk 12), Antigua and Casillas del Angel. I don't think this itinerary is worth the extra kilometres, especially as some of the ground is covered in Car tour 1. However, if you're going to Jandía, use this route to see the enormous U-shaped valleys beyond Caleta de Fuste. Visit, too, Pozo Negro (▲✕), an out-of-the-way fishing village sprinkled across a lava tongue — a 17km (return) detour. Some 3km down the FV420 to Pozo Negro is the turn-off for La Atalayita★ (🎏), an aboriginal village with over 150 prehistoric dwellings and a small interpretation centre.

town on León y Castillo (on the right-hand side of the church), then Juan de Bethencourt (Exit B). This leads to the FV10 to La Oliva. A gentle ascent across a stony plain brings you up to the old airport, Los Estancos, and you drive straight through it. Entering a grand U-shaped valley, you pass through **Tetir** (38km), a well-spread farming village. The enclosing hills are eroded and rocky, bare of vegetation. Montaña Aceitunal (686m/2250ft) dominates the valley with its sharply-pointed features. Climbing out of this valley, you reach a higher one and come into the pretty village of **La Matilla** (43km ✕). Another prominent mountain of equal proportions over-shadows the village: Montaña Muda (689m/2260ft).

Descending from this basin, meet a junction at 45km and bear left on the FV207. The sprawling farming community of **Tefía** (51km **M**) sits on the edge of a vast plain. Behind it rises an amphitheatre of hills. Just beyond the small 'La Alcogida' eco-museum, turn off down the first road forking right beyond Tefía (the FV221 signposted for Las Parcelas/Los Molinos). Just over 1km along, a restored windmill rises on the right. It was used to grind *gofio*, an important food source on the island. The restoration of all these windmills was financed by the EU.

Wine-coloured *cosco* patches the arid flat. You pass through the village of **Las Parcelas**, a farming settlement built after the construction of the nearby (but out of sight) Embalse de los Molinos — a reservoir visited on Walk 8 from Llanos de la Concepción. Dipping down into the narrow and deep Barranco de los Molinos, you come into **Los Molinos** (62km ✕), a tiny fishing hamlet that huddles off a lovely bay encircled by the rock cliffs at the mouth of the *barranco*. If you're going to eat here, *mariscos* (mixed shellfish) is the dish to order. A permanent flow-ing stream that empties out into the sea here, and a pond full of ducks, make this a particularly picturesque spot.

Return to the junction below La Matilla and head left for La Oliva (FV10). Rounding a bend, you look over onto the dark sandy volcano of Montaña Quemada. This particular volcano is rather special because at its base there is a modest monument dedicated to the famous Spanish poet Unamuno, who lived in exile on Fuerteventura.

You next pass above **Tindaya** (81km ✕). It spreads across a flattened crest amidst a profusion of faded brown stone walls. Behind the village stands captivating Mon-taña Tindaya, a great rocky salient that dominates the surrounding countryside with its boldness (see photograph page 63). Looking for the ancient hieroglyphs cut into the rock on the peak (Walk 7) is an adventure in itself.

Just past Tindaya turn right, to ascend to the village of Vallebrón. The road (FV103) winds up and over a pass, before dipping down into the valley. Just over the pass a track veers off sharply right. If you follow it a few hundred metres uphill, you can park and enjoy an expansive view of Tindaya and the surrounding countryside. Rounding a bend in the *barranco*, you look straight up to **Vallebrón** (86km), a cluster of houses cosily set in a hollow amidst thick clumps of prickly pear and stone walls. Short walk 6, a good leg-stretcher, starts and ends here.

Leaving Vallebrón, keep left, then go right immediately at the fork that follows. Fields line the valley floor all the way downhill. Out of the valley, meet a junction and turn left on a narrow road to the country village of **La Oliva★** (93km ✝🏔🍴🅿M and swimming pool). Keep straight along to a T-junction, where a left turn leads to the Casa de los Coroneles and a right turn to the church. The village rests on the edge of a lava flow. Montaña Arena, a mountain of sand, rises up out of the lava in the background. La Oliva was a town of some importance in the 17th century, when the island's military post was stationed here. The official residence was the colonels' house, the **Casa de los Coroneles** (*P*5; photograph pages 56-57), where Walk 5 starts and ends. The refurbished building, opened in 2006 by King Juan Carlos and Queen

Sofia of Spain, is open Tuesdays to Saturdays from 10.00 to 18.00 (entrance fee). To the left of the building stand the dilapidated servants' quarters and stables. One can't help but notice the perfectly-shaped Montaña del Frontón rising up in the background of this naked setting; in fact, it's not the isolated cone it appears to be in the photograph on page 55, but only the tail of a long ridge. The parish church at La Oliva, Nuestra Señora de la Candelaria, overpowers the village with its solid black-stone belfry (photograph page 61); this is where Walk 6 ends, having climbed from Tindaya via Vallebrón. The Casa del Capellán (chaplain's house), another old building, sits off the side of the Corralejo road, on the left. This house, and a small house in the village, which has a stone façade with an Aztec motif, are other examples of the as yet unexplained Mexican influence seen on Car tour 1 at Pájara church. If you're interested in contemporary Canarian art, be sure to visit the 'Centro de Arte Canario' (Casa Mané; open Mon-Sat from 10.30-14.00).

From La Oliva make for El Cotillo*. From La Oliva's church, cross the Corralejo road and follow a narrow village road, soon joining the FV10 for El Cotillo. The FV10 road runs alongside pale green lichen-smeared *malpais;* the fields are fenced off with neat and trim stone walls. Montaña Arena, on your right, makes a noticeable landmark. Follow the lava flow all the way to **El Cotillo** (110km ▲✕; Walks 2 and 4). This once-quiet little port,

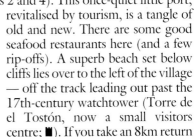

revitalised by tourism, is a tangle of old and new. There are some good seafood restaurants here (and a few rip-offs). A superb beach set below cliffs lies over to the left of the village — off the track leading out past the 17th-century watchtower (Torre de el Tostón, now a small visitors centre; ■). If you take an 8km return

*Another day you might like to take an alternative route back to base, via Caldereta. This quiet little village has some excellent examples of traditional architecture, from simple farm dwellings to comfortable villas. To get there, return the way you entered La Oliva but, at the turn-off for Vallebrón, keep straight ahead on the FV102.

View through American aloes to Montaña Arena, from the Casa de los Coroneles

Left: molina *at Agua de Bueyes; right:* molino *at Valles de Ortega*

detour out to the lighthouse, you will find exquisite little coves ensconced in the dark lava coastline (**P**2; photographs pages 42-43 and 48).

On your way back to Corralejo, you come to a roundabout some 8km along and take the FV109 to the very traditional village of **Lajares** (118km ✕). Walk 3 (my favourite hike on the island) starts here. This charming rural settlement lies amidst a maze of dark lava-stone walls. To see the two windmills for which the village is renowned, take the road forking off right from the next roundabout. A couple of minutes along, this road passes between the two roadside mills. The slender construction is called a *molina:* a wooden contraption that rotates and is built onto the rooftop of a house. The house normally has a room on either side of the mill. More robust is the *molino:* it's conical and is moved by pushing the long arms, thus rotating the cap with the windmill blades. This building is not inhabited. Both mills were used for grinding *gofio*. The photographs above, although not taken at Lajares, will help you identify them.

From Lajares, the FV109 takes you to the FV101, where you go left — or first turn *right* for approximately 1.5km, then follow signs to the Cueva del Llano (∩**M**), a volcanic tube near Villaverde. There is a small museum and an excellent guided tour of the cave (daily 10.00-18.00). On your left the dramatic volcanic scenery of Walk 3 unravels its humps and hollows, and the bold red-tinted sentinel of Montaña Bayuyo (photograph page 51) heralds the end of the tour at **Corralejo** (130km).

✿ Walking _____

Fuerteventura is a large island, but it does not present a great variety of landscapes to the casual visitor. So I hope you will be pleasantly surprised by the many picturesque corners found on these walks which cover a good cross-section of the island. *There are walks for everyone*.

Waymarking and maps

Waymarking has improved by leaps and bounds, and new trails are being developed all the time. Two excellent websites for information are www.magrama. gob.es/en (key in 'Fuerteventura nature trails') and www. spiritoffuerteventura.com (click on 'walking'). Both sites have maps covering the nine stages of the 135km-long **GR131**, which runs from the island of Lobos to Punta de Jandía; it's waymarked red/white. There are also many day walks: **PR trails** (*pequenos recorridos;* day walks, waymarked yellow/white) and **SL trails** (*senderos locales;* 'local' walks under 10km long, waymarked green/white). The *style* of waymarking is the same on all trails: single or parallel stripes indicate 'continue this way'; right-angled stripes herald a 'change of direction'; 'X' means 'wrong way'. These websites don't just list the trails: they describe what you can expect to see, mark the routes on OS-style maps or overlay them on Google maps, show elevation profiles *and* include downloadable gpx and klm files. We've added all these routes (known at time of writing) if they fall within the area of our walking maps.

The **maps** in this book have been adapted from maps of the Servicio Geográfico del Ejército, and heavily up-dated in the field. For GPS users we have overlaid a UTM (28R) projection with 1km grid squares, Datum WGS84. Maps of the island at either 1:50,000 or 1:25,000 are available on order from your local stockist.

Where to stay

There are two main resorts: **Corralejo** in the north and **Morro Jable**, with its string of accompanying resorts, in the south. Two lesser resorts are growing apace: **Costa Calma** at the northern end of the Jandía Peninsula, and **Caleta de Fuste** in the centre. The latter offers fairly good bus access to walks at both ends of the island.

Several seaside villages have apartments if you're travelling independently: try El Cotillo, Las Playitas, Gran Tarajal, Tarajalejo, La Lajita, Giniginamar, and La Pared. But remember that finding unreserved accommodation in high season (Christmas through Easter) is difficult.

There are also more than a dozen **rural hotels and guest houses**, which I heartily recommend. For information log on to www.ecoturismocanarias.com/uk.html.

Puerto del Rosario, the capital, has a few hotels and some *residencias*. Finally, there's also the old *parador,* now in private hands and called 'Hotel Fuerteventura Playa Blanca', just outside Puerto del Rosario.

What to take

If you're already on Fuerteventura when you find this book, and you don't have any special equipment such as walking boots or a rucksack, you can still do some of the walks — or buy yourself some equipment in one of the sports shops. Don't attempt the more difficult walks without the proper gear. For each walk in the book, the *minimum* equipment is listed.

Please bear in mind that I've not done *every* walk in this book under *all* weather conditions. Use your good judgement to modify my list according to the season!

You may find the following checklist useful:

- walking boots (which must be broken-in and comfortable)
- waterproof rain gear (outside summer months)
- long-sleeved shirt (sun protection)
- bandages and band-aids
- plastic plates, cups, etc
- anorak (zip opening)
- spare bootlaces
- sunhat
- insect repellent
- small rucksack
- up-to-date transport timetables
- lightweight water containers
- extra pair of socks
- long trousers, tight at the ankles
- protective sun cream
- knives and openers
- lightweight fleece
- plastic groundsheet
- torch, whistle, compass
- mobile phone (the emergency number is 112)

Weather

Fuerteventura has a climate to match its beaches: the average temperature is 19°C, with fairly hot summer days and a very mild winter ... to say nothing of a healthy

2900+ hours of sunshine per year! But the desert-like climate means that — especially in the north and centre of the island — it can be quite chilly in the evening, *even in summer*.

November to March are the best walking months. Sunseekers, I'm sorry to say that you will get cloudy days, some quite miserable and fresh — just right for a long hike. Wet days — from the blessed (for the islanders) west- to southwest winds — are quite a phenomenon here; they arrive about as frequently as a real summer in England (when everybody remembers the year…).

The main winds are the northeast to north, which can be very strong in spring and summer — just right for windsurfing, and the bothersome southeast to south — a dry hot wind off the Sahara that fills the air with dust. These winds can last for up to five days, and are very unpleasant. In summer, mists (from the trade winds) are common over the Jandía mountains, but they won't affect your beach days. So really, all you've got to worry about is the sun and the heat. Don't overdo it on your first day!

Dogs and other nuisances

With the increase in affluence and corresponding increase in crime on the island, many people now keep **dogs** — not just one dog, but in some cases, two or three. These dogs are there to guard the property, and they do a darned good job of it! I have tried to warn you on walks where you may have problems. Goatherds' dogs are usually all bark and no bite. If dogs worry you, you might like to invest in a 'Dog Dazer' — an easily-portable electronic device which emits a noise inaudible to the human ear but startles aggressive dogs and persuades them to back off. These are most easily and inexpensively obtained online from Amazon.

Usually, where there are goats and sheep, you find **ticks** as well. Fuerteventura is no exception, but because there isn't much long grass on the island, they are less of a nuisance here than elsewhere.

Beach north of El Cotillo

Spanish for walkers and motorists

In the tourist centres you hardly need know any Spanish. But out in the countryside, a few words of the language will be helpful, especially if you lose your way. It may also help you 'break through' the natural reserve of the Fuerteventurans.

Here's an — almost — foolproof way to communicate in Spanish. First, memorise the few short key questions and their possible answers, given below. Then, when you have your 'mini-speech' memorised, always ask the many questions you can concoct from it **in such a way that you get a 'sí' (yes) or 'no' answer.** *Never* ask an open-ended question such as 'Where is the main road?'. Instead, ask the question and then suggest the most likely answer yourself. For instance: 'Good day, sir. Please — where is the path to Tindaya? Is it straight ahead?' Now, unless you get a 'sí' response, try: 'Is it to the left?'. If you go through the list of answers to your own question, you will eventually get a 'sí' response, and this is more reassuring than relying solely on sign language.

Following are the most likely situations in which you may have to practice your Spanish. The dots (…) show where you will fill in the name of your destination. Ask a local person — perhaps someone at your hotel — to help you with place name pronunciation.

Asking the way

Key questions

English	Spanish	approximate pronunciation
Good day, sir (madam, miss).	Buenos días, señor (señora, señorita).	**Boo**-eh-nohs **dee**-ahs, sen-**yor** (sen-yor-ah, sen-yor-ee-**tah**).
Please — where is	Por favor — dónde está	**Poor** fah-**vor** — **dohn**-day es-**tah**
the road to …?	la carretera a …?	lah cah-reh-**teh**-rah ah …?
the footpath to…?	la senda de …?	lah **sen**-dah day …?
the way to …?	el camino a …?	el cah-**mee**-noh ah …?
the bus stop?	la parada?	lah pah-**rah**-dah?
Many thanks.	Muchas gracias.	**Moo**-chas **gra**-thee-ahs.

Possible answers

English	Spanish	approximate pronunciation
Is it here?	Está aquí?	Es-**tah** ah-**kee**?
there?	allá?	ayl-**yah**?
straight ahead?	todo recto?	**toh**-doh **rayk**-toh?
behind?	detrás?	day-**tras**?
right?	a la derecha?	ah lah day-**ray**-chah?
left?	a la izquierda?	ah lah eeth-kee-**er**-dah?
above?	arriba?	ah-**ree**-bah?
below?	abajo?	ah-**bah**-hoh?

Asking a taxi driver to take you somewhere and return for you, or
asking a taxi driver to meet you at a certain place and time

English	*Spanish*	*approximate pronunciation*
Please —	Por favor —	**Poor** fah-**vor** —
take us to …	llévanos a …	l-**yay**-vah-nohs ah…
and return	y venga buscarnos	ee **vain**-gah boos-**kar**-nohs
at (place) at (time).	a … a … .*	ah (place) ah (time).*

*Just point out the time on your watch.

Organisation of the walks

This book describes hikes and rambles all over the
island. To choose a walk that appeals to you, you might
begin by looking at the touring map inside the back cover.
Here you can see at a glance the overall terrain, the roads,
and the location of the walks. Flipping through the book,
you will see that there is at least one photograph for every
walk.

Having selected one or two potential excursions from
the map and the photographs, turn to the relevant walk.
At the top of the page you will find planning information:
distance/time, grade, equipment, and how to get there. If
the grade and equipment are beyond your scope, don't
despair! *There's almost always a short or alternative version
of a walk,* and in most cases these are less demanding. If
you want a really easy walk, you need look no further than
the picnic suggestions on pages 12-13.

When you are on your walk, you will find that the text
begins with an introduction to the landscape and then
turns to a detailed description of the route. The **large-
scale maps** (all 1:50,000) have been annotated to show
key landmarks. **Times** are given for reaching certain
points in the walk. *Note: I am a very fit walker,* and these
are 'neat' walking times. If you prefer a more leisurely
pace, and you stop to picnic or take photographs, a walk
may take you more than twice as long. *Do* compare your
pace with mine on one or two short walks, before you set
off on a long hike. The most reliable way to use this book
is not to try to match my times throughout the walk, but
to use the time checks from one landmark to the next.
Don't forget to take bus connections into account!

Below is a key to the symbols on the walking maps:

▬▬▬	main road	🖅	best views	Å	pylon, wires
═══	secondary road	✚	church.chapel	▪	specific building
═══	tracks	† ✛	shrine.cemetery	🚗	car parking
2→	route of the walk and direction	⌁	spring, tank, etc	🚌	bus stop
2→	alternative route	*P*	picnic spot (see pages 11-14)	⁙	A-A lava
				◡	pahoehoe lava

Walk 1: AROUND LOBOS

Distance: 10km/6.2mi; 2h45min

Grade: easy, but there is no shade, and it can be hot, windy and dusty. The ascent of Montaña La Caldera is just over 100m/330ft.

Equipment: comfortable walking shoes, fleece, sunhat, suncream, picnic, plenty of water, swimwear

How to get there and return: ⛴ from Corralejo to/from Lobos. There are several boats sailing to Lobos, with different schedules (see page 126). If you want to spend the day, take the old ferry called 'Isla de Lobos', a friendly traditional boat; it returns at 16.00. But if you want to return around 14.00 (which will still enable you to do the entire walk and climb the volcano), take the glass-bottomed 'Celia Cruz', which returns earlier (see www.islalobos.es). Note that the Visitors' Centre and adjacent WC open immediately after the arrival of the 10.00 ferry and usually close promptly at 15.00. There are no other facilities on the island.

You can have Jandía and El Jable; I'll settle for Lobos any day. A 35-minute — and sometimes rough — ferry ride with amiable seafarers takes you over to this strange little island of sand and rocky mounds. Seen from Corralejo, Lobos may not even arouse your curiosity. But once you've seen the exquisite lagoon cradled by Casas El Puertito and you've climbed the crater, then finished your day with a dip in the turquoise-green waters off the shore, you'll remember it as one of the most beautiful spots you've visited. Lobos takes its name from the seals that once inhabited these waters. The island is only 3km off the coast of Fuerteventura and measures just 6.5 sq km.

You follow a track that circles the island. A quad, which belongs to the park rangers, is the only vehicle you'll

encounter. On Lobos all the paths and tracks are very clearly marked — *with signs warning you not to leave the marked route: Lobos is a bird sanctuary and a protected area!* Straight off the JETTY, **start out** by forking right twice, to head for the tiny port of Casas El Puertito, a jumble of buildings with a restaurant. A neat wide path leads you there through a landscape dominated by mounds of lava and littered with rock. These small mounds, called *hornitos* ('little ovens'; see page 121) are caused by phreatic eruptions. You'll see the beautiful *Limonium papillatum,* with its paper-like mauve and white flowers. And fluorescent green *tabaiba* glows amidst the sombre rock. You'll also notice plenty of *cosco (Mesembryanthemum nodiflorum),* the noticeably bright red ice plant, and *Suaeda vera.* A reef of rocky outcrops shelters the lagoon, making it into a perfect natural swimming pool. Through the rock you can see the sand dunes of Corralejo in the background; **Casas El Puertito (7min)** is a picture postcard setting. (Tip: if you want to eat here after your walk, order your meal now!)

Once past the little houses, continue around the LAGOON. Almost at once, swing back inland and, at a T-junction, head left. To the right is a coastal path: if you take it, you can rejoin the main walk once you reach the tidal pools.) *Arthrocnemum fruticosum* (a fern-like plant) grows in the hollows. Ice plants (see page 47), with transparent papillae resembling water droplets, also catch the

attention. This plant was once traded for its soda content. The track loops its way through these miniature 'mountains'. The rock is clad in orange and faded-green lichen. Overlooking all this is Montaña La Caldera (the crater), the most prominent feature in this natural park.

Shortly, cross a sandy flat area. The track loops up the embankment; a small fork off to the left cuts the loop and joins the track at an INFORMATION BOARD. Lanzarote begins to grow across the horizon. Ignore the forks off to the right (**30min, 37min**). (The second fork leads

Left: the hornitos *of Lobos — an intriguing landscape. These phreatic eruptions come about when underground water heats up and expands.*

Montaña La Caldera is home to a large seagull colony: take time to observe the fascinating social behaviour of these beautiful and elegant birds.

past a patch of sisal — an aloe-like plant with exceptionally tall flower stems, sheltering in a hollow just a few minutes away.) Soon (**55min**), ignore side-paths to some ugly concrete buildings. Then join a track coming in from the left.

In a few minutes you're alongside the abandoned building and outhouses of the **Faro de Martiño** (**1h10min**). If you don't plan to climb the crater, this will

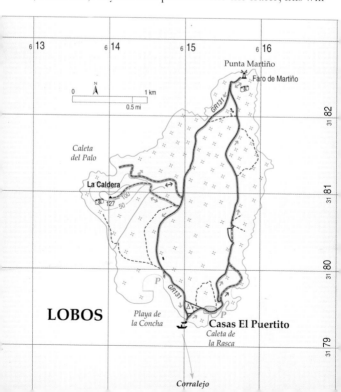

be your best viewpoint in the walk. You look out over the dark lava hills and the tiny valleys of golden sand that thread their way through them. To the right of the broken-away crater of Montaña La Caldera you'll glimpse Corralejo. Across the straits, just opposite, lie some of Lanzarote's magnificent beaches, from Playa Blanca to Punta Papagayo.

From the lighthouse follow the main track off to the right (the GR131). Within 30 minutes from the lighthouse (at about **1h40min**), you will turn off to climb Montaña La Caldera, by taking the *second* fork off to the right. (But first you might like to take a 30 minute return detour to Caleta del Palo, a beach inside Montaña La Caldera's crater. If so, take the *first* right turn (where a signpost points forwards and backwards, but *not* to the Caleta del Palo) and follow the track along a sandy depression. *(Careful: in late spring and early summer breeding seagulls around here can be very aggressive!)* Pass a water tank and continue on a path through a narrow 'valley' of rock, which leads down to this black-sand beach. Return the same way.)

The **Montaña La Caldera** turn-off comes up four minutes after the detour route. Straight into this track, the route forks. Go right and follow the well-worn path that ascends to the RIM OF THE CRATER (**2h10min**). A brilliant sight awaits you. You find yourself on a razor-sharp ridge, looking down sheer walls onto a beach, hidden inside this half-crater. Your vista encompasses the profusion of *hornitos* that make up this island, the dunes of Corralejo, and Fuerteventura's hazy inland hills. To the north, you can trace Lanzarote's coastline as far as Puerto del Carmen. The crater is also home to a large seagull colony. The birds here are apparently used to visitors, as they were not aggressive.

Returning to the GR track, head right. Fifteen minutes after joining the track, watch for the turn-off to the main beach: it comes up two minutes past two concrete buildings that sit in a hollow on your left. This exquisite bay (**Playa de la Concha**; **2h30min**) is actually a shallow lagoon that curves back deeply into the coastline. Here's where you'll end up passing the rest of the day, no doubt. Keep an eye on the departure time of your boat! To return to the ferry, just continue along the track, keeping right at the fork, to reach the JETTY at **2h45min**.

Walk 2: CORRALEJO • MAJANICHO • EL COTILLO

Distance: 22km/13.5mi; 5h20min

Grade: easy but very long. *NB:* Can be very hot, windy and dusty; choose your day carefully.

Equipment: hiking boots preferably (otherwise stout shoes), fleece, sunhat, raingear, suncream, swimwear, picnic, plenty of water

How to get there: 🚐 to Corralejo (Lines 06, 08)
To return: 🚐 from El Cotillo to Corralejo (Line 08), then ongoing 🚐 to Puerto del Rosario if necessary (Line 06)

Short walk: Caleta del Marrajo — Caleta Beatriz — Caleta del Marrajo (9km/5.6mi; 2h25min). Easy; equipment as above, but strong shoes will suffice. Access: 🚗 to/from the water cistern south of the Faro de Tostón, where the coastal track turns off to the right. Park here (everyone does), but *be warned:* there have been some thefts from cars. Use the map to walk to **Caleta Beatriz** and back.

Note: The entire course of this walk can be done in a jeep, since it follows a track. But if you attempt it in your rented car be careful! While the first part is in excellent condition, the second half is sometimes covered in loose sand. Remember the wording of your hire car contract: no venturing off sealed roads is covered by insurance! Note also that a highly-recommended cycle excursion of 28km follows the route Corralejo — Majanicho — Lajares — Corralejo. It's shown on our maps. The first 8.5km is on a bumpy dirt track. Avoid cycling on windy days! Cycles are available for hire in Corralejo.

Even though this hike takes little more than five hours, I recommend you make a whole day of it. Leave fairly early before it gets too hot, take lots of swimming breaks, and be in El Cotillo to catch the five o'clock bus back. The last section of the walk will *wow* you with its white sand coves and limpid turquoise waters embraced by dark jagged arms of lava. With civilisation behind you, you head into a no-man's land, crossing a vast sea-plain — at times meandering through rough seas of lava and at times through dunes. Wherever you look, there are stones and rock and plains stretching for miles in all directions. But just when you're getting tired, another alluring cove appears. Do this hike during the week, when there will be less local traffic (mainly surfers). The jeep safaris and 4WD-tourists are unavoidable, but they by no means ruin the walk.

   Start out from the BUS STATION in **Corralejo**. Head north down the road to the sea. Just past the bus station, turn

Approaching the Faro de Tostón

42

left on a dirt track signposted to Majanicho (exit C on the town plan on page 10). Setting out, the most prominent landmark is Bayuyo (Walk 4), the volcanic cone on the left with a gaping crater. Ascending slightly, you have an uninterrupted view of Lanzarote and its built-up coast-line. Playa Blanca is the resort directly across from you. And back to your right is the little 'pimply' island of Lobos, littered with small volcanic mounds. On the left side of the track you look out over *'malpais'* (badlands) lava ... and are soon swallowed up in it. Stone walls in varying stages of decay criss-cross this landscape, and volcanic cones rise out of it. Apart from succulents and small thorny bushes *(aulaga)*, little other vegetation survives here. Rock and stones cover the ground. The landscape appears dark and subdued, until a closer look at the *malpais* reveals varying shades of green lichen plastered across it, and the jagged rock is a mass of turbulent humps and hollows.

You'll pass a few lone fishermen's shacks; then, at **1h50min** more or less, a small rustic settlement comes up. Crossing a rise, Majanicho, which still about 15 minutes away, comes into sight. This charming retreat of little weekend houses encircles a narrow shallow inlet with a small sandy beach. At **Majanicho (2h05min)** a road branches off left for Lajares (the route recommended for cyclists) and the large tourist development of El Jablito; keep straight ahead.

Beyond Majanicho the terrain briefly becomes sandy,

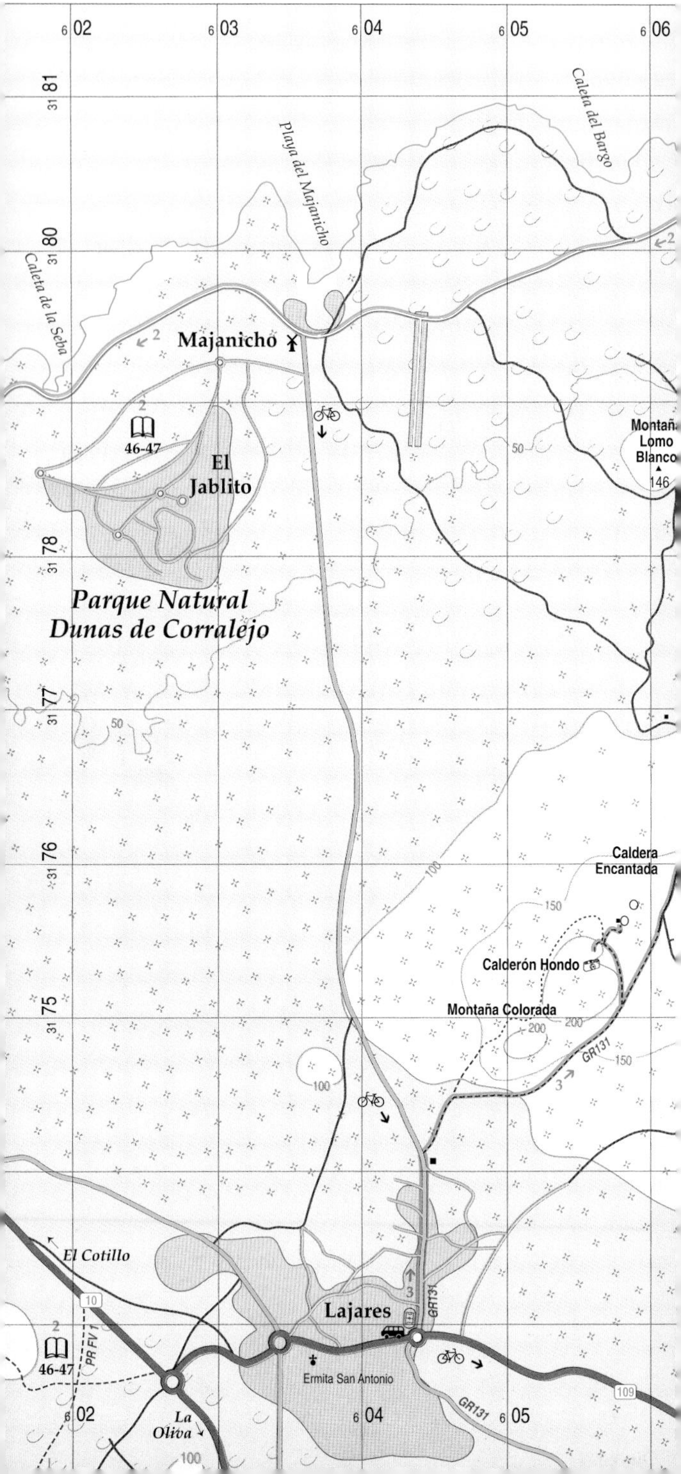

Caleta del Bargo

Playa del Majanicho

Caleta de la Seba

Majanicho

2

46-47

El Jablito

Montaña Lomo Blanco
146

50

Parque Natural Dunas de Corralejo

50

100

Caldera Encantada

150

Calderón Hondo

Montaña Colorada

200

GR131

150

100

3

El Cotillo

46-47

PR FV

10

2

Lajares

3

GR131

Ermita San Antonio

GR131

109

La Oliva

100

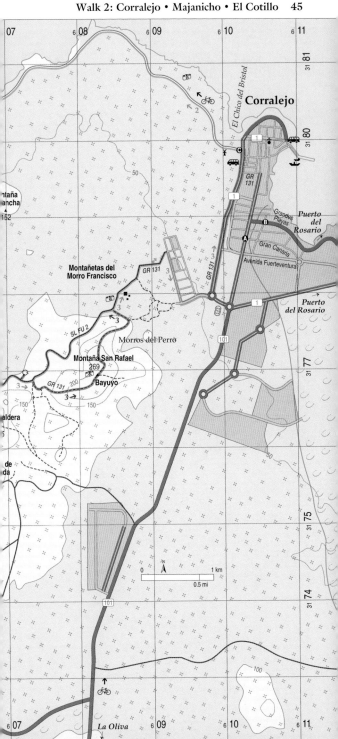

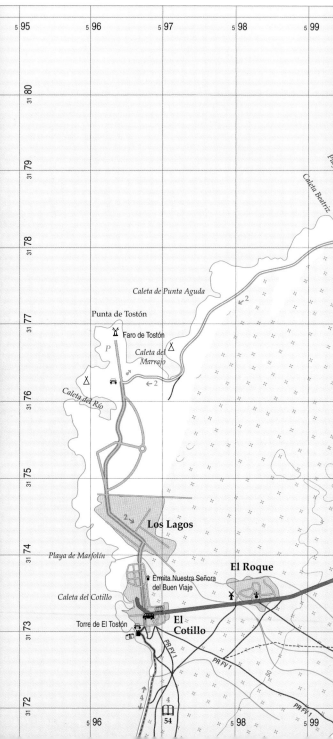

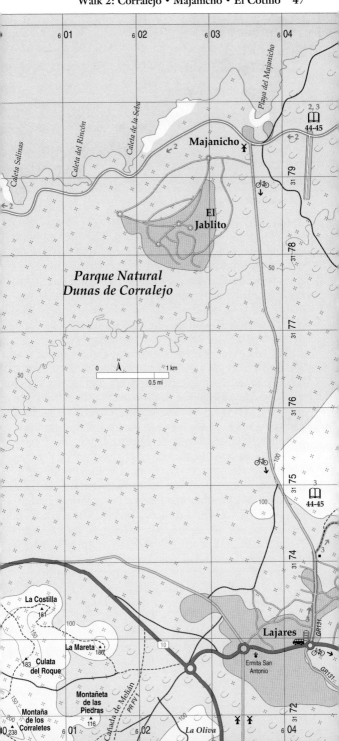

Playa del Castillo, just south of El Cotillo

and you pass behind another beach. This is a popular surfing spot, but the beach itself is very rocky, hence no good for swimming. Just past the beach a short ascent gives you a bird's-eye view back over it — and there's still time to change your mind if you think I have underestimated it. My favourite swimming spot lies a little further on. Just before it, you pass a smaller inlet with a couple of beach shanties — also a nice swimming spot.

The track circles behind *my* beach, **Caleta Beatriz**, at **3h15min** into the walk. It's the deepest of the inlets so far. The water is an irresistible green, and there's a nice slab of sand at the end of it. Moreover, nobody seems to stop here. The next bay seems more popular — perhaps because it's not quite so close to the track. The lighthouse at Punta de Tostón is now an obvious landmark.

Nearly an hour further on, a biggish bay (Caleta del Marrajo) stretches across in front of you, with the lighthouse at the far side. It's a beautiful stretch of coastline. Jagged arms of rock jut out into the bay, creating lagoon-like pools. Sand dunes roll back inland. The track forks behind the bay, so be sure to keep right, along the shore. Towards the end of the bay the track climbs towards a stone water cistern just beyond which you reach the ROAD FROM EL COTILLO TO THE LIGHTHOUSE (**4h20min**).

Turning left, follow this road for 4km. Coming into **El Cotillo** (**5h20min**), keep straight on along Avenida Los Lagos until you reach a T-junction with the Lajares road by the sports ground. Turn left here. The bus leaves from in front of the telephone transformer building on the next corner (*not* from the bus shelter behind the building).

Walk 3: FROM LAJARES TO CORRALEJO — THE CRATER ROUTE

See map pages 44-45   **Distance:** 14km/8.7mi: 3h05min

Grade: moderate, with a steady 160m/525ft climb at the outset

Equipment: comfortable walking shoes, light jacket, sunhat, raingear, suncream, picnic, plenty of water

How to get there: 🚌 to Lajares (Lines 07, 08)
To return: 🚌 from Corralejo (Lines 07, 08)

Shorter walk: Lajares — Calderón Hondo — Lajares (10km/6.2mi; 2h 40min). Easy; equipment as above. 🚌 (Lines 07, 08) or 🚗 to/from Lajares. Follow the main walk to **Calderón Hondo**; return the same way.

Definitely the most interesting walk on the island. Those of you interested in vulcanology will have a field day. And even if you couldn't give a hoot about volcanoes, it's *still* a brilliant walk — especially done late in the afternoon. In spring, you'll be surprised by the amount of greenery in this harsh landscape.

Start out from the BUS STOP in **Lajares** next to the FOOTBALL GROUND. Head north on the road at the right of this stadium (CALLE MAJANICHO, also the red/white waymarked GR131). Follow this road for 10 minutes (1km/.62mi). Then, just past the last house on the right, turn off on a wide path signposted 'CALDERON HONDO'.

Your way is exquisitely cobbled and bordered by stones on both sides — a work of art. Surrounded by a lichen-covered *malpais,* ignore a faint path to the left and head straight towards a dark brown volcanic mound, **Montaña Colorada**, which rises boldly in front of you. The path skirts the foot of this volcano, then ascends to an elevated plain. Magnificent stone walls stretch across the inclines below. The next volcanic mound to appear on the left is Calderón Hondo. Don't forget to look behind you and appreciate the view over Lajares. Crossing a crest, you pass through a wall. To the right you look out over the sand dunes of Corralejo, separating the dark lava flow and the blue sea.

On coming to a fork at the base of **Calderón Hondo** (**50min**), head uphill to the left. After five minutes ignore two paths forking off to the right very close together; continue steeply uphill to the left, to the VIEWPOINT (**1h 02min**). An impressive crater lies below. A surprising amount of vegetation grows on and out of the rock here. You have excellent sea views to both the left and the right. Majanicho (Walk 2) is the small seaside village seen to the left. The plains below are littered with corrals and dotted with buildings, many of which lie abandoned.

Now head back to the two forks you passed on your

49

The herders' hut on Calderón Hondo is obviously a replica, but its thatch and mud roof, with supporting beams and lava stone walls, paint a vivid picture of their way of life.

way to the *mirador:* they are now descending on your left. Take the second turning. Minutes along, you come to the traditional HERDERS' STONE BUILDING shown above. The small stone conical-shaped construction to the right was used for cooking. A corral, also made of lava stones, stands nearby. The setting merits the few minutes' detour.

Return to the point where you turned off to the *mirador,* and now head left towards Corralejo. Crossing this elevated plain, you look into **Caldera de Rebanada**, the collapsed crater on your right. Five minutes later, a track cuts across in front of you. Follow it (still the GR131) to the left downhill towards a hamlet of scattered buildings. Ignore a track forking left* and continue straight on towards Corralejo. You can now safely ignore all turn-offs and just follow the track (first the GR131, then the green/white waymarked SL FU 2) along the foot of the volcanoes. **La Caldera**, another prominent volcanic cone, overshadows you on the right. Heading into an undulating landscape of lava, the way now ascends, and

---

Recommended detours: Ten minutes after this junction, a clear path to the left leads in under a minute to a hole in the lava — a volcanic gas bubble which has split open. Some 200m/yds past the 'bubble path' the GR131, marked with cairns, heads right and climbs to the summit of Mt Bayuyo. After 20 minutes you reach the top of the lower ridge, 10 minutes more takes you to the trig point. Ignore the path down off to the right from this trig point; continue left along the ridge. The descent is steep and slippery in places. When you reach the bottom of the mountain, take the trail to the left, before the stone wall. This takes you back to the track where you can pick up the notes below. Allow 40 minutes extra for this detour.

Above: from the ferry off the shore of Corralejo, it's easy to trace out the end of the walk. Bayuyo is the gaping crater dominating the background. Right: view into Calderón Hondo's crater from the mirador.

you twist and wind through hillocks and depressions. Amidst the stone and rock there's a surprising amount of greenery about in spring — if the island's been blessed with the normal February rains.

Forty minutes along the track, you cross a crest and dip into the gaping crater of **Bayuyo** (**2h05min**), a landmark for miles around Corralejo. This amphitheatre of mountain is about to encompass you when your way swings off left. You pass some abandoned sheds and stables and one or two illegal tips. Soon after, rounding a bend in the hillside, Corralejo comes into sight (but it's not as close as it looks!) … and a corner of Lobos.

Descending, and out of the lava, you pass a large white water tank on the left and turn right in front of a failed housing estate with only a couple of properties. At the end of the development, turn left at the T-junction. Coming to the roundabout on the main FV1 dual carriageway, turn left (still with the GR; see plan on page 10). Follow this straight on for just under 2km, to the BUS STATION on the left (**3h05min**).

51

Walk 4: EL COTILLO — THE CLIFFTOP WALK

Distance: 11km/6.8mi: 3h

Grade: easy, mostly along the clifftops. The descent down steps to the sea may be unnerving for some. *Note:* don't walk too close to the cliff-edge, it could crumble away beneath you! And on windy days keep even further away from the edge of the cliffs. No shade.

Equipment: comfortable walking shoes, swimming things, fleece, sunhat, raingear, suncream, plenty of water

How to get there and return: 🚌 to/from El Cotillo (Lines 07, 08) or 🚗 (park at the watchtower, Torre de El Tostón)

Apart from the superb sea views, what delighted me most on this hike were the barbary ground squirrels. Yes, feeding them bits and pieces from my lunch. Doing just the kind of thing they ask you *not* to do in the parks, where the signs all read 'please don't feed the squirrels'.

The hike starts from the 17th-century WATCHTOWER (**Torre de El Toston**, also called Castillo de Rico Roque). It's currently a tourist information centre, where contemporary art exhibitions are also held. From the tower you overlook a long sandy beach that rests at the foot of dunes. (If travelling by bus, head for the coast and turn left to the tower.) Beyond the beach rise sheer cliffs. The hike will take you along this beach, before you mount the cliffs and head along them. No matter what time of day you start out, you'll see surfers out on the waves.

Follow the track behind the tower, heading south. A

couple of minutes along, at a fork, descend the crest and start making your way along the beach. On windy days, which are common, sand gets blown into every orifice! (Always remember: the beaches on this side of the island are dangerous because of undertows. People do swim at this beach, but *don't* venture out far.)

When you reach the END OF THE BEACH (**30min**) climb to the clifftops above. Now up on the sea-plain, just follow the cliffs — a faint track is traced out along the top. It's part of the PR FV 1. Looking back, you can see El Cotillo across from you, and inland, the small village of El Roque. Apart from a few lone buildings, there is little sign of life inland. Smooth denuded hills rise back off the plain.

The coastline with its sheer cliffs keeps your attention. Below, you can see a shelf of submerged rock extending quite far out into the aquamarine sea. Within **1h** you're overlooking a big bite in the shoreline — the long sweep of **Playa del Aguila**. From the clifftop here look towards the cliffs in the latter half of the 'bite', and you should be able to see steps down to the sea — your immediate destination. Some minutes further along, a small sandy beach appears at the foot of the cliffs below.

Large photograph: looking back to El Cotillo from the top of the steps above Playa del Aguila. Right: the barbary squirrels are much loved by 'Landscapers', who even bring them titbits.

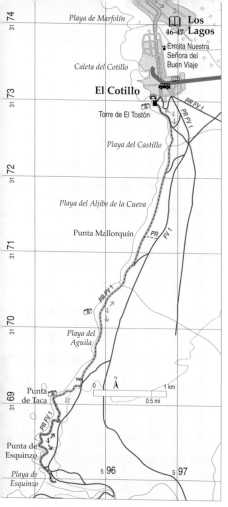

A little over 10 minutes later, you're at the top of the STEPS (**1h 15min**). Just before you descend, you have a beautiful view back along the coastline to El Cotillo, and in the distance you can see the lighthouse at Punta de Tostón. Some people may find the descent unnerving, but the steps are very sound. Beyond the stones at the foot of the steps, you can see the sandy seabed. The sea looks very tranquil, and it's quite shallow. I've never swum here, nor have I seen others do so, so take extra care if you do try these waters.* This is also where you'll find the squirrels … on the clifftops and along the rocky shoreline. (You needn't find them, they'll find you!)

Climb back up the steps and, before heading back to the watchtower, walk along to the right for 10 minutes — over to the next small HEADLAND, **Punta de Taca** (**1h40min**), where you'll find a well-placed bench overlooking another fine sea view. From here the main walk heads back the same way to **El Cotillo** (**3h**), but if you've another hour or so in hand, why not continue along the the cliffs to the information board where PR FV 1 begins, at Playa de Esquinzo?

*If you want to walk to the small beach overlooked earlier, it lies 10 minutes along to the right — *but if you walk there, keep your eye on the tides.*

Walk 5: LA OLIVA • MORRO CARNERO • LA OLIVA

See map pages 58-59; see also photograph pages 30-31

Distance: 6.2km/4mi; 2h50min

Grade: strenuous, with a tough, steep 300m/1000ft ascent over stony and rocky terrain. Descending is equally strenuous, due to the loose stones underfoot. Some cross-country walking with no path.

Equipment: hiking boots, sunhat, light jacket, rainwear, suncream, picnic, plenty of water

How to get there and return: 🚌 (Lines 07, 08) or 🚙 to/from La Oliva. Drive or walk to the Casa de los Coroneles (signposted from the church), to begin the walk.

Alternative walk: La Oliva — Morro Carnero — Vallebrón — La Oliva (11.6km/7.2mi; 4h30min). Grade, equipment and access/return as main walk; ascent/descent of 400m/1300ft. Follow the main walk to the top of Morro Carnero (1h40min), then walk back along the ridge but, instead of descending, continue along the ridge. In about seven minutes you reach another small rise. You can see your ongoing path on the side of the next slope, ahead and on the left, skirting this mountain. Descend to a pass with two old stone corrals on the left, then take a faint path on the left 50m/yds past the corrals. This skirts the flanks as a goats' trail, then peters out. Keep contouring for about five minutes, then start to descend — *slowly and carefully, keeping to the bedrock wherever possible*. Descend to the rocky plateau below you, then pick up the disused path you saw earlier, just below the plateau. Follow this to the right.

The perfect cone of Montaña del Frontón, seen through palms at the start of the walk

Keep contouring round the hill when this path fades away, then zigzag down to the gully and cross it. On reaching the first houses in Vallebrón and coming on to asphalt, continue down to the Centro Socio Cultural (2h40min). From here pick up Walk 6 at the 1h30min-point and follow it to the end.

Both this walk and the Alternative walk are only recommended for the adventurous. If you want similar views without all the huff and puff, do Walk 6 instead. In this hike, or rather climb, the summits will afford you the best panorama over the north of the island.

Start out from the **Casa de los Coroneles**. This old manorial house, refurbished and re-opened in 2006 by King Juan Carlos and Queen Sofía of Spain, is one of the 'sights' of the island. The still-dilapidated buildings at the left were the servants' quarters and stables. Your destination is the highest point of the ridge behind the building, seen in the photograph below. (Before the walk you might like to see inside the house: it's open Tuesdays to Saturdays from 10.00 to 18.00; a small fee of 3 euros is payable.)

Facing the building, walk round it to the right. Climb over some rubble and loose stones, to pick up a wide, slightly overgrown path bordered by stone walls. Follow this towards a ruined homestead, a few minutes away. Walking through an archway that's seen better days, you're soon standing beside the homestead. A small water catchment lies to your right, and a row of palms in front

of you beautifies this otherwise barren spot. To your left stands the perfect cone of Montaña del Frontón.

You now cross the abandoned fields in front of you. Within a couple of minutes, on reaching a gravel track, follow it to the left. Ploughed fields below the track stretch back to the hills. A few minutes along the track, you meet a property enclosed by a high wire fence. Walk to the end of the fence and head right, up through the fields, towards the foot of the mountain, following the fence uphill. When the fence 'ends' by turning away to the west (**40min**), just make your own way up to the crest, crossing a hillside covered in loose stones and rock. Now the ascent begins! Looking out over La Oliva, you get a taste of the views to come. Montaña Arena (photograph pages 30-31) is the bigger of the two volcanic mounds in the background, each of which is encircled by a bib of *malpais* criss-crossed with stone walls.

Approaching **1h30min** into the hike you're on the TOP OF THE RIDGE — more than likely being blasted by the wind. From here you have an unsurpassed 360-degree panorama of the north. Your views sweep out over La Oliva to El Cotillo slightly to the left (through the volcanic mounds) and a corner of Corralejo, with the volcanic island of Lobos beyond it. Filling the horizon to the right is Lanzarote. On the south side of the ridge, you look down into a narrow valley. It hides the small farming settlement of Vallebrón — still mostly out of sight because

it's tucked up into the hillside. Walk 6 would take you straight up this rarely-visited valley. Facing La Oliva, now walk along to the right for 10 minutes, to **Morro Carnero**, the end of the ridge (**1h40min**).

Return the same way, giving yourself plenty of time and heading down the hillside slowly and carefully, back to the **Casa de los Coroneles** (**2h50min**).

The Casa de los Coroneles, with Morro Carnero rising at the left of the ridge in the background.

Walk 6: TINDAYA • VALLEBRON • MIRADOR DE TABABAIRE • LA OLIVA

Distance: 11km/6.8mi; 3h20min

Grade: moderate-strenuous ascent of 200m/650ft, but any fit person will be able to manage it. The 15-minute descent from the *mirador* is steep and skiddy; you must be sure-footed and have a head for heights

Equipment: hiking boots, light jacket, sunhat, raingear, suncream, picnic, plenty of water

How to get there: 🚌 to Tindaya (Line 07)
To return: 🚌 from La Oliva (Lines 07, 08)

Short walk: Vallebrón — Fuente and Mirador de Tababaire — **Vallebrón** (5km/3mi; 1h20min). Moderate, with a steady climb of 100m/330ft. Equipment as main walk, but comfortable shoes will suffice. 🚗 to/from Vallebrón; park at the Centro Socio Cultural, in the village centre. Follow the main walk from the 1h30min-point to the *mirador* and *fuente*, and return the same way.

The *mirador* visited on this walk is one of the best on the island, yet hardly anyone knows about it ... if you exclude the jeep safaris. This is the one negative point about the walk, but the safaris don't go up there every day. And the hidden valley that cradles Vallebrón is also little

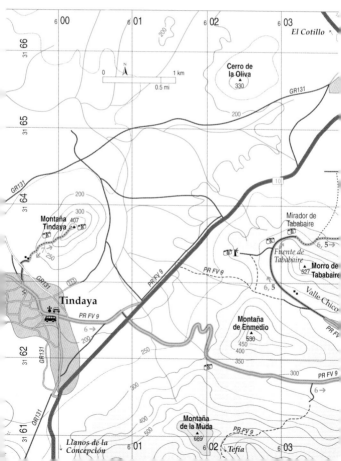

visited. (But if road-walking is not your 'thing', you could use the map to follow the PR FV 9 northeast alongside the FV10 for 500m and then to the right — either all the way to Vallebron and out again, or just to the track in the Valle Chico, where you would turn left for the *mirador*.)

Get off the bus at **Tindaya**. To **start the walk**, follow the departing bus, heading east along the road (towards La Oliva). About 1km along you will come to a sign denoting the end of Tindaya. Just past this sign walk to the right, 125m/yds across a field, to reach the MAIN ROAD (FV10; **20min**). Then cross the road and continue on the Vallebrón road opposite.

You now follow this road, which only sees local traffic, to Vallebron, over an hour away. A steady climb will take you up and over a pass hemmed in by craggy peaks. A little over 1km uphill, once the pass is crested, a welcoming avenue of palms leads you down towards the village nucleus. The valley walls sweep back into razor-sharp ridges, and remains of terracing step the walls. Deep

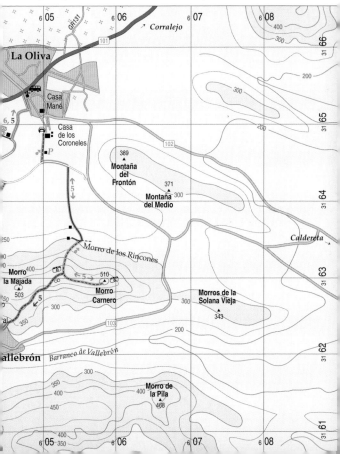

Watering hole at the foot of Montaña Tindaya; note the wine-red cosco *in the foreground.*

in this silent valley, after rounding a bend, you look up into a huddle of houses set into a hillside hollow. Bibs of prickly pear sit around the houses, and the gardens are a riot of colour. Just below **Vallebrón** a track forks off the road to the left by a small TRANSFORMER STATION. Take this short-cut and, a minute later, when you come out on a road, turn left uphill to the **Centro Socio Cultural** (**1h30min**). *(The Short walk begins here.)*

Continuing on, take the road above the cultural centre and go left, ascending into another valley (Valle Chico). Stone walls border the road, which reverts to gravel after 10 minutes, when you pass the last house. At a fork that follows, keep right. You will remain on this track all the way to the *mirador,* ignoring all turn-offs. This is goat country, and you pass a corral with adjoining sheds and yappy dogs! Montaña Tindaya (Walk 7) and its surrounding village creeps into view as you ascend.

Around 35 minutes uphill, pass a fork off left to a telecommunications aerial. (If you take this 15 minute detour, you will be rewarded with a fine outlook over Tindaya and surroundings). Then a spectacular view unravels. La Oliva, a small farming settlement, sits in the middle of a patchwork of fields. An ochre and black

60

View just before reaching the Mirador de Tababaire — a fine outlook over the outskirts of La Oliva, with Montaña Arena rising in the background to the left. Below: church at La Oliva

volcanic cone called La Arena stands boldly behind it. And on a clear day this superb panorama is made complete with Lanzarote filling the background, and a deep blue sea stretching to the horizon. A little further on, when you get to the *mirador,* you will be able to sit down and just soak it all up. The gravel track reverts to dirt as you pass the **Fuente de Tababaire** (**2h10min**), a couple of small water troughs cut into the rock face — a water source for the animals. The **Mirador de Tababaire** is just a minute further on. *(The Short walk turns back here.)*

To continue the main walk, take your bearings: you now make your own way over open terrain, down the hillside and across the plain below, aiming for the Casa de los Coroneles, a large gold-coloured building slightly to the right. When you reach the bottom of the mountain and the animal fence that surrounds it, turn right alongside the fence. Walk through a gully and then head in a straight line towards the Casa de los Coroneles, hopping through gullies every now and then. When you reach the corner of the fence again, skirt to the right of it until you meet a track. Follow this to the left, past the school and into **La Oliva** (**3h20min**). The BUS STOP is on the main road — just past the church, outside a pharmacy.

Walk 7: MONTAÑA TINDAYA

Map pages 58-59   **Distance:** 3.8km/2.4mi; 1h45min

Grade: a strenuous, but short, pathless ascent of 220m/720ft up a very steep, rocky mountain. This hike is difficult for inexperienced walkers and would be dangerous in wet or very windy weather.

Equipment: walking boots, fleece, sunhat, suncream, raingear, picnic, plenty of water

How to get there and return: 🚌 (Line 07) or 🚗 to/from Tindaya. Alight from the bus in the village, where the bus turns round; park by the church.

Important note: Permission is needed to climb to the Tindaya summit, which is under protection. A sign in Spanish warns that you should not climb above 300m without a permit, and a ranger will be there to check that you have one. The permit must be collected in advance from Medio Ambiente (the environmental conservation agency) in Puerto del Rosario: Calle Lucha Canaria 112 (8 on the town plan; open Monday to Friday 08.00-14.00; tel: 928 861115; take your pasport). You will be allocated a time slot between 08.30 and 11.00 for the climb. If you read Spanish, you can apply for the permit online at www.cabildofuer.es/portal/RecursosWeb/DOCUMENTOS/1/1_1236_1.pdf.

Montaña Tindaya is no ordinary mountain. Not only is it a prominent feature in the landscape, but the Guanches regarded it as their holy mountain. On its summit they slaughtered young goats and offered these sacrifices to their gods. A number of important relics from the Guanche epoch have been found on the mountain, and rock engravings can still be seen around the summit.

Off the bus in **Tindaya**, **start out** by following the main road west past the CHURCH SQUARE (the best place to leave your car). This peaceful farming settlement curves around the gentle slopes of a sprawling hill. The houses are scattered amidst garden plots, which sit behind stone walls criss-crossing the inclines. Goats and sheep doze in their pens. Here on Fuerteventura the goats are quite a breed. Some nannies are able to give as many as eight litres of milk over a 24-hour period! Past the church, the road curves round to the right. Now Montaña Tindaya stands before you; its sheer inclines make the summit appear inaccessible.

Minutes below the church you go straight through a junction, then pass a CHILDREN'S PLAYGROUND and an ELECTRICITY SUB-STATION, both on your left. Some 40m/yds past the latter, turn right on a tarmac road. A minute along, fork right uphill on a gravel track. When you reach a T-junction, turn left. Then, at a FINGERPOST after only 30m/yds, go right — heading up to the TWO DERELICT STONE COTTAGES in front of you, at the base of the hill. Your ascent begins just behind them, where you climb the tail of the ridge. A path briefly marks the way.

Montaña Tindaya, from the start of the walk

The ground is stony and carpeted in wine-coloured *cosco* (see photograph on page 60) and ice plants. When food was scarce in years gone by, the dried fruit of the *cosco* plant was used to make an ersatz *gofio* (an important food source on the island, usually made from roasted corn). The fallen fruit of the *cosco* was collected and ground into powder. Although there is no longer a path, the ascent is very straightforward: stick to the top of the crest all the way. Above the gravel you come onto bare rock.

At about **1h** you reach the SUMMIT. (The crest topples off onto the plains below not far beyond it, so take care!) You have a fine view of the surrounding countryside. On clear days you can see Lanzarote; El Cotillo is the village ensconced in the coastline over on the left, and La Oliva is the sprinkling of white straight ahead off the end of the mountain. Immediately below, on the left-hand side of the mountain, sits a picturesque homestead surrounded by gardens and a lean palm grove — a pretty picture in this harsh landscape.

Now for the treasure hunt. Most of the ROCK ENGRAVINGS are around the summit. The easiest to find are the two on an upright, smooth rock face just below the summit (on the eastern, or village side) — within a radius of some 5 to 8 metres (15 to 25 feet) from the top of the peak. Others are located on the next clump of rock further along the ridge. Once you've found one, you soon find the others. *Suerte!* Unfortunately, some of them have been defaced.

Descending the mountain is slow going. A lot of care is needed. Allow yourself enough time to return to the bus, if you didn't come by car. You should be back at the church in **Tindaya** at **1h45min**.

Walk 8: LLANOS DE LA CONCEPCION •
EMBALSE DE LOS MOLINOS • MORRO DE LA CUEVA
• LLANOS DE LA CONCEPCION

Distance: 13km/8mi; 3h20min

Grade: moderate. Much of the walk is pathless and over stony terrain. It can be very hot, and there is no shade. A 300m/1000ft ascent.

Equipment: walking boots or stout shoes with ankle support, fleece, sunhat, suncream, raingear, picnic, plenty of water

How to get there and return: 🚌 (Line 02) or 🚗 to/from Llanos de la Concepción; park at the Bar García.

The Embalse de los Molinos is the largest reservoir on Fuerteventura. Its water level varies from year to year. Recently it has been unusually dry and the surrounding vegetation had either died off or been eaten back by goats. Hopefully the water level will rise over the coming years.

Setting out from **Bar García**, take the road that runs down into the village (with the bar on your left). For the first 40 minutes you'll head towards the conical hill ahead, then your way will swing left, before you ascend the hills over to your left to return to the bar/café. Llanos de la Concepción, a scattering of houses, is deep in slumber. Clumps of prickly-pear and a few thick-leafed aloes sit behind the tired walls. Much of what was once cultivated now lies fallow. A road joins from the left, you pass through an INTERSECTION where you briefly join the GR131 and, two minutes further on, when the road forks (outside a shop), you keep straight ahead, now on a track. Another track joins from the left a few minutes later, followed by a road after another minute. Follow this road down into a gully, where you cross a stream bed.

You head across a vast valley, its left side lined by smooth worn hills and its right side bordered by *cuchillos* (Spanish for 'knives': these are younger and sharper hills). The terrain is stony and dry. Solitary cultivated corners make a sharp contrast in this ochre-coloured landscape, with their vivid greenery. In spring scarlet poppies and daisies run amok in the gardens, and the plain is smeared with cereal-like *Gramineae*. You pass straight through another INTERSECTION (**20min**) and later ignore two turn-offs to the left. There are some modern houses in this area, with natural sandstone walls.

Approaching the **40min**-mark you again enter the STREAM BED, just as it joins another coming from the right. A faint track goes left here. Metres/yards along, you leave the stream bed and the main track as well, ascending a track forking off to the left. You immediately pass a small farm building on the left (ignore the track entering the

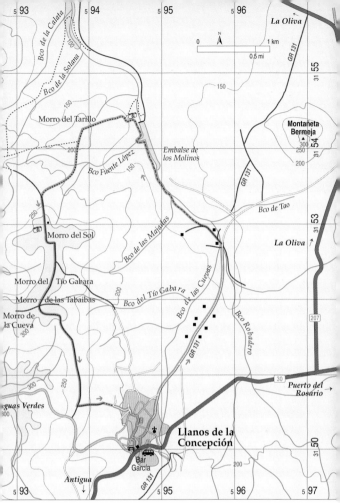

gully to the right here). A large, modern farmstead lies up ahead — emitting a horrendous smell! Ignore a few minor tracks going off left and right. Soon a FIRST FENCE blocks your way. Go through the gate (making sure it's properly closed afterwards), or clamber over it. When the way swings up left to an old, abandoned farmhouse, keep straight ahead, following the *barranco* and crossing through a dense colony of ice plants and *cosco*.

You catch sight of the dam wall up ahead and gradually the tail of water below grows into a muddy brown reservoir. If you're into ornithology, go quietly: birds do congregate around the muddy end of the dam here. The last time I came I saw dozens of coots. Continuing round the **Embalse de los Molinos**, you'll need to scramble up the rocky slopes and make your way around the inclines

Sharing the ridge above Llanos de la Concepción with some goats. The 'Great Wall' can be seen in the background, the fencing in the foreground.

above it — one of the most attractive spots on the walk, where asphodels covers the slopes.

Around half an hour from the last fence you encounter a SECOND FENCE (**1h15min**). Follow it down to the edge of the reservoir. Now, if the water level is high, you won't be able to skirt it ... without disappearing into the mud! In which case you'll have to follow the fence up onto the headland for a few minutes, to where you can climb over it (there are stones on either side of the fence to help you). If the water level is not too high, make your way around the bottom of the fence, *first testing how soft the mud is!* Once you've rounded the fence, an arm of water in a small side-barranco needs skirting. This is also a good spot for bird-watching, and you may see some herons. Keep around the edge of the arm of water and then ascend the side of the ridge. *Again, check any mud you intend to cross before ploughing straight on!* Descending to the dam wall needs careful footwork; the hillside is steep and gravelly.

From the DAM WALL (**1h30min**) scramble up onto the top of the crest above the dam, from where you'll have a good view over the reservoir and across the valley to the impressive barrier of hills. A small village (Colonia García Escamez) of white block houses lies near the end of the valley. Red *cosco* stains the surrounding inclines, and a hint of green lies in the sheltered folds. The serenity and isolation of this landscape has a beauty all its own.

Home is now over the hills you've just circled. With your back to the barranco just below the dam, head for the nearest round-topped hill, following a faint track that heads slightly left but then veers right near the top. From here, head for the highest peak visible: you may be able to see a wall descending from the top (from this angle it may look more like a dyke), and there is a ruined stone shelter part way up that you will pass on the ascent. Descend the rough ground and, about 30 minutes from the dam wall, you cross the STREAM BED that runs between the two ridges (**2h**).

Now aim for the shoulder to the right of the peak. When you reach it you come onto a faint two-wheeled track and look straight out over another valley. Continue up the track to the left. Near the top of the crest you pass the STONE SHELTER seen previously and soon the coast comes into view on your right. Close on **2h30min** you reach the second hilltop, **Morro de la Cueva**, the highest point in the walk (358m/1175ft). It's near the 'Great Wall' of Llanos de la Concepción (an impressive stretch of wall along the top of the ridge). Inland lie bare desiccated hills, climbing one upon the other.

Remaining on the track, pass through the wall and follow it along the top of the ridge, to the right. Two minutes along you pass through the goat fencing once more (the wire-mesh gate may be hard to see at first; make sure it is securely fastened behind you). Llanos de la Concepción is now in sight below. Valle de Santa Inés huddles high in the hills ahead. Ignore a track going off the mountain here. Close on 15 minutes beyond the wall, your track swings up left onto a lateral ridge, heading towards Llanos de la Concepción, while the wall and the fence continue to the right. More of Santa Inés opens up — and terracing, stepping shallow *barrancos*.

Some 20 minutes downhill, with a road not far ahead, leave the track and descend left to the village on a fainter track (where there may be a goat enclosure). Walk cross-country for some 70m/yds, to a clear track lined by a stone wall. When you hit asphalt, use the map to make your way past the school and back to the **Bar García** (**3h20min**).

Windmill and haystacks at Llanos de la Concepción

Walk 9: FROM ANTIGUA TO BETANCURIA

Distances: 5.5km/3.5mi; 1h50min

Grade: fairly strenuous, with an ascent of 340m/1120ft, much of it up a stony path

Equipment: walking boots, sunhat, light jacket, suncream, picnic, plenty of water; raingear in winter

How to get there: 🚐 to Antigua (Line 01)
To return: 🚐 from Betancuria (Line 02)

Alternative walk: Betancuria — Degollada Vieja — Betancuria (3.5km/2.2mi; 1h20min). Grade and equipment as main walk; ascent/descent of 200m/650ft. 🚐 (Line 02) or 🚗 to/from Betancuria. This straightforward climb is very rewarding — a good, if demanding, leg-stretcher on a car tour. From the bus shelter below the church at Betancuria, walk south on the FV30 towards Vega de Río Palmas. Just 50m past the Valtarajal Bar-Restaurant, turn left on the white/red/green waymarked GR131/SL FV 29 and head straight uphill (see map).

This is the pilgrim's walk. Every year on the third Saturday in September hundreds of pilgrims make their way across these hills to pay homage to the Virgen de la Peña in Vega de Río Palmas. The contrast you'll see in vegetation is reason enough to do the hike. In winter there's a rare lushness on the hilltops rarely seen on this island, and grass abounds.

The walk begins at the leafy SQUARE in **Antigua**. With the belfry behind you and the square on your left, head along the street (CALLE VIRGEN DE ANTIGUA). After a minute, at the junction, turn right (there should be a fingerpost here for the SL FV 29). Go through another junction and soon cross the valley floor. Palms border the road. Ignore two roads to the left and, shortly after, a road to the right. Within **10min** you'll see a WATER TANK on the right, and two roads forking left. Take the second road to the left, which goes straight ahead towards the barrier of hills cutting across in front of you. You can see your ongoing route from this point — a wide path ascending a lateral crest not far ahead, offset slightly to the right.

Around 10 minutes later ignore a road to the left. Some 90m/yds further on, when the road forks right, continue straight ahead on a track. Garden plots lie fallow on the left. Just below a CONCRETE SHED with a TANK, the way forks. Head right up the wide SL FV 29 path, the ascent now noticeable. A lush little cultivated valley unravels to your left and, looking back down over the scattering of Antigua, you have a sweeping view. Low volcanic humps and razor-backed ridges stretch across the horizon.

A SIGN designating the area *'parque rural'* comes up just over **30min** en route. You zigzag your way uphill towards the crest. Nearer the top, the spiny *aulaga* bushes give way to bright green *tabaiba*. The path fades briefly, but traces of stone walls come to the rescue. In winter low cloud may brush the ridges. The terrain gets rockier, and the greens of the *verode*, *tabaiba* and asphodelus bring life to these otherwise insipid slopes. Then the grass becomes noticeable; the landscape softens. Quite a treat! Soon goats and sheep will keep you company.

Crossing the **Degollada Vieja** (also called Degollada del Marrubio or Degollada de la Villa; **1h20min**), brace yourself for a blasting on windy days! A brilliant sight awaits you now, as the vegetation changes completely. The inclines are dotted with wind-battered pines, and grass carpets the ground. Straight below lies Betancuria, ensconced in these hills. Keeping straight over the crest, you descend on a very wide path. Thick leathery-leafed aloes border the path and nearby fields. Baying dogs

Betancuria, with the 17th-century cathedral church of Santa María

Church at Antigua (top), climbing from Antigua to the Degollada del Marrubio (middle), grassy slopes and wind-battered pines on the descent from the pass to Betancuria. Right: landscape near Antigua. The windpump at the right is used for drawing water from sunken wells (see notes on page 18).

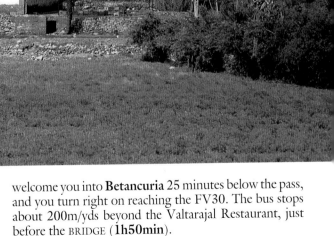

welcome you into **Betancuria** 25 minutes below the pass, and you turn right on reaching the FV30. The bus stops about 200m/yds beyond the Valtarajal Restaurant, just before the BRIDGE (**1h50min**).

Walk 10: BARRANCO DE LAS PEÑITAS (VEGA DE RIO PALMAS)

See also photographs on pages 12, 17

Distance: 5km/3mi; 2h (or 8.4km/2h45min for those travelling by bus)

Grade: quite easy, but the path to the chapel could prove unnerving for those prone to vertigo. *Be very careful if it's wet!*

Equipment: comfortable shoes or walking boots, fleece, sunhat, suncream, raingear, picnic, plenty of water

How to get there and return: 🚌 (Line 02) or 🚗 to/from Vega de Río Palmas. Motorists travelling south on the FV30 should turn right just under 400m past the church at Vega de Río Palmas on the narrow road to the reservoir; park by a bridge at the entrance to the path/track into the stream bed. Those who come by bus should alight at the church and walk 50m/yds downhill, then turn right by a walkers' information board on a track leading into the dry stream bed. Follow the stream bed to the left, then a tarmac road, to the bridge where the walk begins.

Alternative walk: Barranco de las Peñitas — Ajuy — Playa del Jurado — Ajuy (12.5km/7.8mi; 4h20min). Moderate; equipment as above, but walking boots are recommended. SL FV 06. Access by 🚗: arrange for friends (or a taxi) to drop you off at the starting point for this walk and collect you again at Ajuy. Follow the main walk for 50min, until it turns back. Here scramble down over the boulders for a few minutes, keeping left. You'll cross a big water pipe, from where it's easier to get down to the floor of the **Barranco de las Peñitas**. Once down in the bed of the *barranco*, keep straight ahead, entering another *barranco* (**Barranco de Mal Paso**) cutting down in front of you. Descend this *barranco* (ignoring all farm tracks left and right), crossing a road in about 40min. After about 1h10min you will spot a small valley chock-a-block full of palms cutting back into the hillside on your right (the **Barranco de la Madre del Agua** — see photograph pages 76-77). *Do* go and investigate it. Then return to the main *barranco* (now the **Barranco de Ajuy**) and continue down to **Ajuy**, where you can pick up Walk 11.

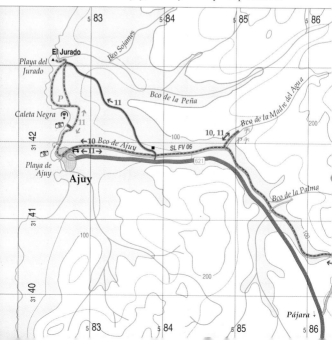

This stroll is short and sweet; it takes you down one of the island's most picturesque valleys, the Barranco de las Peñitas. Palm trees dot the valley, and a small reservoir rests in the floor. From the reservoir wall you look through a corridor of rock out onto more palms and salubrious garden plots far below. In winter you may find dark green pools embedded in the floor of the barranco. Hidden in the sheer walls lies the delightful little Ermita de Nuestra Señora de la Peña — just the kind of place where one might feel inclined to offer up a prayer.

Start the walk in **Vega de Río Palmas** at the BRIDGE over the **Barranco de las Peñitas**: take the gravel track that strikes off right just before the stream bed and drops down into the dry stream bed (SL FV 06/27). A healthy sprinkling of tall palms graces the valley floor and indeed, the entire valley. For Fuerteventura, this is the height of arboreal luxury! Abrupt craggy ridges dominate the landscape. Follow the stream bed until, a little over **10min** off the road, the ways climbs up right out of the *barranco* on a wide old washed-out track. When the track forks, go left, skirting the reservoir. This track quickly becomes a narrow trail. A sign indicates that this area is a bird sanctuary.

The valley floor quickly fills with tamarisk and then forks. The left-hand fork swings back up into the hills; the right-hand fork cradles the reservoir, before folding up into a narrow ravine that drops down to join the Barranco de Mal Paso. You're surrounded by hills, with the pointed

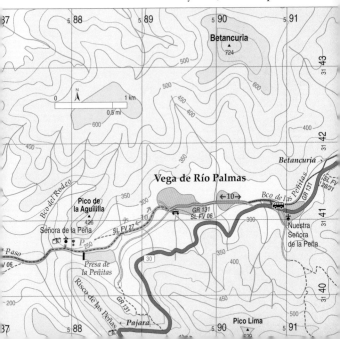

The Presa de las Peñitas from the FV30; the chapel is just visible above the dam. Below: Nuestra Señora de la Peña, with the palm-choked Barranco de Mal Paso below

Gran Montaña (708m/2320ft) dominating the valley. The now-narrow trail winds amidst large boulders. Soon the *presa* is just below you — murky green in winter and spring, probably bone dry in summer. Green garden plots set amidst palm trees terrace the slopes on your left now. The *barranco* is freckled with verode — the brightest plant on the slopes. Less than 10 minutes along, you're on the RESERVOIR WALL (**30min**). The bare escarpment stares down on you, as the ravine closes up into a deep V, before emptying out onto an oasis of palms and gardens and continuing its seaward journey.

Beyond the reservoir wall you follow a stone-paved path that has been built into the sides of the *barranco*. Parts of this path have crumbled away, requiring steady footwork … and the lizards darting about are distracting. The pools may be no more than puddles by the time you visit, but they *can* be very deep. A couple of minutes down the path, you spot the tiny white chapel of **Nuestra Señora de la Peña**, perched on a rocky outcrop above the stream bed. A short stretch of path leads to it. This path clings to the face of the rock and is quite unnerving, but it's fairly short — only some 30m/yds.

Inside the chapel you'll find bits of clothing, plastic flowers, and a visitors' book that makes for interesting reading. On a scorching hot day, the chapel provides the

perfect retreat for a picnic. Beyond the *ermita* the path hangs out over the side of the *barranco*. This stretch of path might also prove unnerving for those without a head for heights. It's an impressive piece of path-building, that's for sure. Nearing the end of the *barranco*, a few minutes along, the path vanishes. End the walk in this picturesque corner (**50min**).

Returning, follow the same route, remaining on the path just above the reservoir until you re-enter the stream bed. You should be back at the BRIDGE in **Vega de Río Palmas** in **2h**. Those making for the BUS STOP should allow another 25-30min (1.7km) back to the church. The Line 02 bus leaves at 16.30.

Walk 11: AJUY • PLAYA DEL JURADO • AJUY

See map pages 72-73

Distance: 3.7km/2.3mi; 1h30min

Grade: easy, but don't venture too close to the edge of the cliffs — they could crumble away easily.

Equipment: comfortable shoes, fleece, sunhat, raingear, suncream, swimwear, picnic, plenty of water

How to get there and return: 🚌 to/from Ajuy. Park at the turning circle at the entrance to the village, or down by the beach. (Bus line 04 serves Ajuy, but timings are unsuitable at present.)

Alternative walks

1 **Ajuy — Barranco de la Madre del Agua — Ajuy** (5km/3mi; 1h15min). Grade, access and equipment as above (except for swimwear). From Ajuy walk up from the beach into the **Barranco de Ajuy**. About 40min along you'll come to a small side-valley on your left, crammed with palms — the **Barranco de la Madre del Agua**. It's sheer bliss in the shade of trees here, listening to the trickle of water. Return the same way.

2 **Ajuy — Barranco de la Madre del Agua — Playa del Jurado — Ajuy** (8km/5mi; 2h25min). Grade, equipment and access as above. Combine Alternative walk 1 and the main walk into a lovely circular walk, to make the most of the varied landscapes in this little pocket of Fuerteventura. From Ajuy follow Alternative walk 1 up to the **Barranco de la Madre del Agua**, then retrace your route for 7min. When a track crosses the *barranco*, follow it up to the right, soon passing some ruined houses. Ignore a track off to the right. Shortly after, pass through a rickety fence. Then ignore another track to the right. Some 50min after leaving the *barranco* you reach the beach at **Playa del Jurado**. Now use the map to follow the coast back to Ajuy.

At the mouth of the Barranco de la Madre del Agua — the site of a tiny, permanently-flowing stream. Enjoy Picnic 11a here, under a profusion of palms.

On the main walk you'll be awed by the striking coastal scenery and El Jurado, an impressive rock pierced with a hole. The short 10-minute stretch up to the Caleta Negra *mirador* is in every brochure, so you'll have to share it with half of Europe! But the rest of the walk you'll share with very few. On Alternative walk 1 you see one of Fuerteventura's loveliest palm groves, and in its midst hides a tiny permanently flowing stream — a unique corner of the island.

Start the walk at the TURNING CIRCLE at the entrance to **Ajuy**: descend into the village of dazzling white houses until you reach the black sandy beach which stretches out to the left. Now you ascend a beautiful stone-laid path built into the *barranco* wall on your right. The black-sand beach and the cluster of little white houses make a striking contrast. Rounding the rock wall, you come upon a spectacular view: from chalk-white rock terraces (a fossilized beach, a rare geological feature!) you look across a blue sea towards cliffs hollowed out by massive caves. You'll pass every tourist and his dog on this path. When the path forks, take the upper branch; the lower one descends to a coastal platform.

A little over **10min** will bring you to the *mirador* — a viewing balcony in the face of the cliff. The paved steps

down to it are protected by sturdy wooden railings, as are those to two enormous, fascinating caves below the *mirador*. Further steps continue down to the sea, but these are narrow and vertiginous. Take great care if you descend these unprotected steps, especially if it's wet or the sea's rough.

To continue on to Playa del Jurado, head back up the path and veer up to the left, to the clifftops above. Now you've left the crowds behind. A path, partly marked with cairns, takes you along the cliffs and round the shoreline. Cross a gully and come to a fence with a GATE in it. Go through the gate, closing it after you. From this side of the bay you look back towards the *mirador*, to see more

caves carved into the cliffs. It's a spectacular piece of coastline.

With your back to the gate, head straight across this slightly raised flat area. Soon you'll see the jagged tail of a *barranco* wall ahead. Aim straight for it. Playa del Jurado comes into sight — with a monument of rock, Fuerteventura's own Arc de Triomphe, perched at the water's edge. The easiest place to descend to the beach is down the gentle slope just opposite the end of the *barranco* wall — otherwise take the clear track down to the beach (where 'alternative life-stylers' camp from time to time). Tamarisk trees huddle along the valley floor. Unfortunately, cans and bottles have been dumped here, so watch

out for broken glass. At **40min** into the walk you're standing on **Playa del Jurado**. Remember that the beaches here are deadly dangerous!

Return to the gate the way you came or follow the shoreline; timings are about the same, and you will be back at the TURNING CIRCLE in **1h30min**.

Far left and below: landscape at Caleta Negra, near the mirador. *Left: El Jurado, at the mouth of the Barranco de la Peña.*

Walk 12: CALETA DE FUSTE • *LAS SALINAS DEL CARMEN* • *PUERTO DE LA TORRE* • *CALETA DE FUSTE*

Distance: 14.5km/9mi; 3h30min

Grade: easy, mostly along a gravel track, with a brief stretch along the clifftops. Short descent into and out of the Barranco de la Torre.

Equipment: comfortable walking shoes, light jacket, swimwear, sunhat, raingear, suncream, picnic, plenty of water. *Note:* the Restaurant Caracolitos, mentioned below, is closed Sundays (at time of writing).

How to get there and return: 🚐 (Line 03) or 🚗 to/from Caleta de Fuste. (If travelling by bus, add an extra 1km/0.62 mi to/from the beach, where the walk starts and ends.)

Short walk: Caleta de Fuste — Las Salinas del Carmen — Caleta de Fuste (7km/4.3mi; 2h). Easy; access and equipment as above. Follow the main walk to **Las Salinas** and return the same way.

Alternative walk *(closed 15/2-31/7 to protect nesting vultures)*: **Caleta de Fuste — Barranco de la Torre — Caleta de Fuste** (17km/10.5mi; 4h20min). Easy ups and downs; some cross-country walking; access and equipment as above. Follow the main walk to the 1h45min-point, then return to the beach in **Barranco de la Torre** (2h15min). Head up the track into the canyon. When the track veers left to a homestead (2h30min), continue on a faint track in the dry river bed. Buzzards and even Canarian vultures *(guirre)* nest in the walls of the *barranco* on the right. After 35min in the canyon you will see a barbed-wire fence on your right, fencing off a stone quarry (2h50min). Walk alongside the fence for 60m/yds, then take the faint track that leads up to the crest. Once on the top of the crest, follow the line of the *barranco* to the right, walking cross-country. Cross a small canyon and when you meet a track (3h20min) follow it a short way, then cross the FV2. Now head half-right cross-country again, rising after about 300m/yds to a track above a small gully. Follow this to the right and cross the FV2 again at Las Salinas. Here's your second chance to visit Los Caracolitos, before you return to **Caleta de Fuste** along your outgoing route (4h20min).

I have to admit that, for me, this walk doesn't rate as highly as the Restaurant Caracolitos en route. My mouth still waters when I think about the mussels done in garlic and a spicy local sauce that they served up. Ah, yes, the walk… The Short walk (the very popular stretch to the salt pans and the restaurant) makes a pleasant late afternoon stroll, especially if you have a late lunch or snack in mind! The best part of the hike, however, is *beyond* the restaurant, where you dip into a pretty little *barranco* filled with palms and verdant succulents. Then, out of the *barranco,* a magnificent stretch of coastline awaits you, and it's unlikely you'll have to share it with a soul … or even the ubiquitous goat.

Start out from **Restaurant Frasquita**, a restaurant on the south side of the beach. Walk past the Hotel Los Geranios on a promenade, then cross a sandy stretch and pick up the promenade again at the Sheraton Hotel; you will now follow the seaside promenade all the way to the

Hotel Elba Sara, past sea pools, hotels and a shopping centre. Soon arriving at what appear to be restored FORTIFICATIONS, if you climb the tower-like building, do so with care, as the steps are very narrow.

When the promenade ends quite abruptly, walk to the shore to continue. Then pick up a sandy track. After **55min** you come to a road into **Las Salinas del Carmen**, a huddle of white dwellings set on a slope overlooking a small beach and brightly-coloured salt pans. To the left is the Museo de la Sal (Salt Museum), well worth a visit. Now go and find *the* restaurant (the turn-off to it is well signposted). It overlooks the sandy beach, and it's tremendously friendly. *Buen provecho!*

Continuing out of Las Salinas (in company with with SL FV 08 which runs south to Pozo Negro), you cross the beach and then climb a crest on a narrow path beside

View back over the Barranco de la Torre from the stony plain

the ocean. After a few minutes, on reaching a walled-in property, turn right to the road and follow it to the left. The road becomes a track. Over the crest you look down onto the small black-sand beach of Puerto de la Torre, with a couple of derelict buildings, tents and caravans — a popular camping spot. Bright green patches of succulents light up the floor of the **Barranco de la Torre**, and a sprinkling of palms dot the *barranco* a short way inland.

Twenty minutes from the restaurant you're on the beach at **Puerto de la Torre** (**1h15min**). (If you want to take a stroll up through the palms, the furthest stand is only 10 minutes away, but this detour is *not* included in the overall times.) To ascend the *barranco* and continue the walk, take the track veering off to the left. A short steep climb brings you up to a dusty plain littered with stones. Shortly you pass through the gateway of a rather broken down FENCE. Leave the track here, and follow the line of the fence towards the clifftops, five minutes away.

From here on the clifftops become your way, and you pass the remains of some LIME KILNS *(hornos de cal)*. The sea below is a beautiful turquoise-green. Barely 15 minutes along the clifftops you come to the Bimboy TRIG POINT on a jutting promontory (**1h40min**), from where there are beautiful views along the shoreline. Behind you, at the foot of the cliffs, a rocky shelf stretches out, and Caleta de Fuste is visible in the distance. Ahead lies your last port of call on this walk — a small stony beach tucked back into this indented coastline.

A little over five minutes later, a gravel slide takes you down to the beach, at the mouth of the **Barranco de Majada Honda** (**1h45min**). It's a blissfully quiet spot. *Please note:* I have never swum at these beaches, so I do not know how safe they are. If you do intend to go swimming, please do so with the utmost care. As a rule, the beaches on this side of the island are considered safe.

The return follows the same route, and you're back at **Caleta de Fuste** approaching **3h30min**.

Walk 13: FROM GINIGINAMAR TO TARAJALEJO

Distance: 6km/3.7mi; 2h10min (add 4km/1h if travelling by bus)

Grade: moderate, with lots of dipping in and out of *barrancos,* but no climbing to great heights. The path is rough and *vertiginous* — only recommended for adventurous, sure-footed walkers with a head for heights. No shade.

Equipment: walking boots, light jacket, sunhat, raingear, suncream, picnic, plenty of water

How to get there: 🚌 (Line 01, 04, 10) to the Giniginamar turn-off, from where you must walk 4km/1h down the FV525 to the Playa de Giniginamar to start the walk proper. Otherwise, ask friends to drop you off, or take a bus to Tarajalejo and a taxi from there to Giniginamar. *To return:* 🚌 from Tarajalejo (Lines 01, 04, 10)

Short walk: from Tarajalejo to the first beach and return (2km/1.2mi; 1h). Easy, with a short, steep, gravelly descent to beach. Equipment as main walk, but sturdy shoes will suffice; access by 🚌 to/from Tarajalejo (Lines 01, 04, 10).

When you're tired of the beach and feel like getting those muscles working again, then I suggest this wild rugged coastal walk. However, it's not for everybody. If you're not the adventurous type, then the short walk should do nicely.

The walk starts at the BEACH in **Giniginamar**. (There are no buses here, but it's only an hour's walk (4km) down from the turn-off, otherwise take a taxi or ask friends to drop you off.) Head over to the little houses at the water's edge on the right-hand side of the beach, a few minutes along. Your path ascending the side of the ridge starts at the right-hand side of these houses. The steep stony path takes you up to the TOP OF THE RIDGE in **15min**. Now you have a lovely view back over this predominantly fishing village, and back up into the *barranco.*

A little further along the coast opens up. Crests roll seaward and drop off into the sea. More crests and *barrancos* lie ahead, as you wend your way along the coast, dipping in and out of a succession of valleys, roller-coaster fashion. Ignore faint paths down to the sea. Soon you come upon a first (short) stretch of rocky descent down the side of a ridge, but this only takes a couple of minutes. Further along, rounding the next crest, you're over looking a steep drop to the sea. The path is narrow, and would be unnerving for anyone who doesn't have a head for heights.

Just over **30min** into the walk you reach a small stony beach at the mouth of a stream. Another, narrower *barranco* follows. Don't forget to look behind you as you cross here, for a fine view. Small piles of stones have been left to help mark the way … and seagulls have provided the white paint work! Two more small *barrancos* follow, as the still-vertiginous goats' path takes you above the cliffs. It's a harsh environment you're crossing, the only noticeable vegetation being spiny *aulaga* and the odd hawthorne.

Some **55min** en route you encounter your only landmark — a large CONCRETE BLOCK in the middle of the path. Just beyond it another stretch of vertiginous path takes you around the steep face of a hill. A small stony beach comes into sight below a promontory to the left. Here a short steep descent takes you down and across a wide stream bed, the **Barranco del Caracol**. (If you were to go down this stream bed for a few minutes, you would come to the beach at the Punta del Caracol).

Once across the *barranco*, ignore a path to the right. Without warning you're virtually balancing on a clifftop, with a beach stretching out below you. (The fork off left here also goes down to the beach on the point.) Now several vertiginous path lead across the face of the hill: take the widest one (the middle path) and head above the beach; the paths all meet up a minute later. At the end of the beach, a short, slippery descent takes you down to another *barranco* crossing. Out of this (unnamed) stream bed the way veers inland. The fork left is a short-cut along a vertiginous path; keep right. You circle the top of a crest covered in CAIRNS (**1h20min**) — all passers-by have added to the collection. On the crest you meet a track: bear left, descending into the umpteenth *barranco*. A longish, steep ascent follows.

Seven minutes out of the stream bed, when the way

Looking back to Giniginamar near the start of the walk

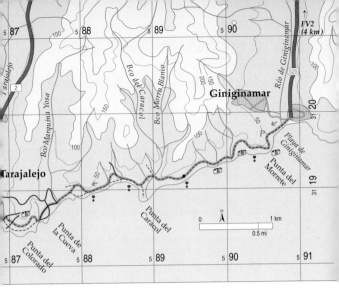

forks, go right, away from the cliffs. Crossing another crest, you spot another beach below. At the fork that follows, descend to the left. This beach is accessible by vehicle, with tents and caravans about. It sits at the bottom of the very wide **Barranco Marquina Yosa**, which fans out as it approaches the sea. Note that these beaches drop away very abruptly into deep water.

At the end of the *playa* your track ascends the hillside. The other tracks here don't concern you. Looking back across valley from here, you suddenly realise how large it is — an amphitheatre of hills circling back to the coast, and within this amphitheatre are more hills and valleys. You cross another track on the top of the crest, and dip down into your last *barranco* and *playa* (**1h45min**), from where you continue on a path. A steep climb takes you out of the *barranco*, and paths fork off in all directions. Basically they're all okay, as long as you don't veer inland, but I suggest the higher path that heads round the hillside, not the one near the shore. Tracks head off here in all directions.

The beach at Tarajalejo appears … then the resorts and the urbanization up in the valley and, finally, tucked into the hillside, the village itself comes out of hiding. After crossing a track, you join another track descending a crest, meet up with the lower path, and head over towards the houses. Coming into the back of **Tarajalejo** (**2h05min**), pick up a street and follow it to the right — to a roundabout on the FV2. The bus stops (for both directions) are just along to the left (**2h10min**).

Walk 14: THE SAND-ENCRUSTED CLIFFS OF THE PARED ISTHMUS

Distance: 12.5km/7.8mi; 3h15min

Grade: easy. The walk crosses a sandy plain on tracks. One steep, slippery descent lasting a few minutes, and a steep 15min climb up a sandhill. Don't attempt on very windy days, when all the sand in the air will make it extremely unpleasant.

Equipment: comfortable walking shoes, fleece, sunhat, suncream, sunglasses, rainwear, picnic, plenty of water

How to get there and return: 🚌 (Lines 01, 04, 05, 09, 10) or 🚗 to/from Costa Calma. The name 'Costa Calma' covers three different resorts: you want to alight from the bus or park at the El Palmeral shopping centre (the bus stop is known as 'Restaurante/Taberna Costa Calma').

Shorter walk: from Costa Calma across the isthmus and back (9km/ 5.6mi; 2h30min). Easy; access and equipment as main walk. Follow the main walk for 1h15min, then return the same way.

You start off this hike with the giant wind generators stealing your attention, then you cross the sandy isthmus to the spellbinding sea and its glaring cliffs and rolling dunes. If you're staying anywhere in the vicinity then this walk is a must. It's a popular excursion, so you needn't worry about finding your way. However, tracks criss-cross this isthmus in all directions, and the route could easily change in the near future. *Basically as long as you **head straight over the isthmus**, you can't get lost.*

Start out at the **El Palmeral** shopping centre. Walk uphill on the road to the right of it. Minutes up, you're away from the resort. In front of you lies a sandy plain that stretches into nothingness. But before you notice anything else, you'll be spellbound by rows of wind generators over to your left. Not only are they a work of art (or perhaps you beg to differ!), but they blend into the landscape. They're striking in their simplicity.

About **6min** along, when the road ends, continue ahead along the middle of three

The spectacular seascape near the point, Los Boquetes

tracks. Far to the right you can see the jagged hills that enclose the Tarajalejo Valley, where Walk 13 ends. To the left, the 'hills' are barely ripples in the landscape. The faint whining sound of the wind generators permeates the air.

You'll see other walkers crossing the isthmus. All on different tracks. But don't panic, you *are* on one of the tracks that will get you there. When you encounter a fork (**25min**), veer left for a closer look at the WIND GENERATORS, and a little over five minutes along you'll be standing just below them. Return from here to the main route and then turn left.

Five minutes on, join a track coming along from the right and keep straight ahead. At the fork that follows, head right, and cross a track. A second track crossing follows. The sea is now in view. After crossing another track you're almost there — perhaps being battered by the wind. The island seems to roll straight off into the sea — the cliffs are still in hiding. To your left is the piercing mountain chain that rears up along the Jandía Peninsula.

Several faint tracks now cross your way and you continue straight on. Beyond one more wide track, you're above the sea, **1h15min** from Costa Calma. A bite in the cliffs allows you to slide your way down to the shore in just a few minutes. A rocky sea-ledge sitting just above the water, at the foot of the cliffs, enables you to walk

PENINSULA DE JANDIA

EL JABLE

Morrete de Veril Manso

GR 131

Degollada de Mojones

Atalayeja
Grande
▲
234

Loma Negra
▲
322

Montañeta de
los Verodes

Bco. Tras del Lomo

SL FV 11

Casas de
Pecenescal

Bco de Pecenescal

El Paso
▲
253

RISCO DEL PASO

Bco del Valluelo

GR 131
SL FV 11

km 73

Bco de Pecenescal

Casas
Risco
del
Paso

Bar

GR 131

Morro Jable

102-103

Walks 14 and 15: at 30min you're standing just below the wind generators. Some of you won't agree with me (especially since they have added a third row since this photograph was taken), but they are one of my favourite sights on the island!

quite a long way along the shoreline. This seascape is exquisite, with its brilliant blue waters, dark lava-coloured rocks and off-white, rose- tinted cliffs of fossilized sand.

Your immediate destination is the point along to the right, where the cliffs subside into sandhills. This coastal walk is nothing short of spectacular. On hazeless days you can see the Jandía Peninsula curving out to your left.

Barbary ground squirrels (see photograph page 53) scurry to and fro amongst the rocks. Not far along you come to a small sandy beach. A knee dip is about all I can recommend here ... it's the usual story: dangerous undertows. Nearing the point, sandhills roll back off the shore. The waves crashing over the shoreline rocks here are an awesome sight. Closer to the point, notice the dark red hues emanating from the sea-cliffs below you. A little under 45 minutes along the sea ledge you're at the point, **Los Boquetes (2h).** A few minutes further on, a dramatic rock wall blocks your way. Don't venture too close to the sea here!

Homeward bound, you have to ascend the sandy hillside behind you. Climb to the highest point to get your bearings. Stunted *aulaga* and large-thorned *espinos* grow rampant on these dunes. Your target from here is the wooded park-like area behind Costa Calma, which is now in sight. Continue straight on along the **Cañada del Río,** the stream bed below, sometimes on a track marked with cairns. Keep to the left side of this canyon or walk through it. Getting closer to civilization, you may have to pass through a fence and then a short tunnel before coming to a small ROUNDABOUT (**3h05min**). Keep straight ahead through the urbanization. On coming to a roundabout just past the Royal Suite Hotel, you'll find the BUS STOP

(for those travelling south) to the right (**3h15min**). If you're heading north, go past this bus stop and, at the following roundabout, go right. Go left at the fourth roundabout, then cross the main FV2. You'll see your BUS STOP ahead, in front of the Hotel Fuerteventura Playa. (If you came by car to Costa Calma, you can either walk the 2km back to the El Palmeral shopping centre by keeping straight ahead at the fourth roundabout, or catch a southbound bus for Costa Calma.)

Crossing the isthmus (Walk 15)

Walk 15: THE DUNES OF THE PARED ISTHMUS

Map pages 88-89; photos pages 90-1
Distance: 13.5/8.4mi; 4h15min

Grade: relatively easy if it's not too windy. Turn back if you encounter strong winds — it will be very unpleasant otherwise, as much of the walk is through sand dunes (and sand sometimes blows over the tracks, hiding them altogether). A drawn out ascent of 170m/560ft. No shade.

Equipment: comfortable shoes, fleece, sunhat, suncream, sunglasses, raingear, picnic, plenty of water

How to get there: 🚌 or 🚗 to Costa Calma (as Walk 14, page 86)
To return: 🚌 (Lines 01, 04, 05, 09, 10) from the Barranco de Pecenescal — back to base, or back to your car at Costa Calma

Shorter walk: Barranco de Pecenescal — Degollada de Mojones — Barranco de Pecenescal (9km/5.6mi; 2h30min). Moderate ascent of 150m/500ft. Equipment as above; 🚗 or 🚌 (as above) to/from the Barranco de Pecenescal (park at the km73 marker on the FV2, by GR131 signboards). *Note:* be prepared for strong winds at the pass!

Unique on the island! A walk through *real* sand dunes, not like the tame dunes at Corralejo. And should you strike a wind, which is the usual case, you'll think you're crossing the Sahara. If heading through a sand-dust storm doesn't sound like your cup of tea, give this hike a miss. I strongly recommend it, however. (The Shorter walk gives you the chance to turn back, if it's far too windy.)

Start out by following Walk 14. At the WIND GENERATOR turn-off (25min), turn left, but almost immediately, turn right on a well-worn, two-wheeled track which cuts across in front of you. Looking across the isthmus to the right, Granillo, a prominent sandy hillock, rises in the northeast. For the moment you're heading towards the sea. Your sandy track is as straight as a railway line.

Keep more or less straight ahead across the isthmus, ignoring forks and intersections (most of them at right angles to the track). Crossing a crest, descend seaward. Bits of the coastline unravel, and sandhills slide off into the sea. Not more than 200m/yds short of the clifftops, cross another track (1h20min) and continue to the edge. Enjoy the spectacular coastal view over sand-encrusted cliffs, lava rock and white-capped waves.

Returning from the cliffs, head right along the track. Ignore all tracks forking down to the sea. On meeting a fork in a few minutes, swing left uphill. If haze or sand dust doesn't obliterate your view, you have a good outlook along the formidable barrier of mountains that run along the peninsula from here. If it's going to be windy, you'll know by now — and it will get much worse once you're crossing the open dunes! A steady climb lies ahead, and you cross a track slicing in front of you. At

1h50min a track joins you from the left, and the way levels out. Rounding a hill, you have an impressive view across the dunes and may be surprised to find grass growing on the hillsides. Just before getting into the dunes proper, it's a good idea to get your bearings from this height, especially if visibility is low and you can't see any of the tracks! (Don't worry. The whole idea is to continue from here approximately parallel to the coast; then, when the sand dunes make way for other terrain — like darker rock — walk 90° inland. This way you cannot get lost.) At a fork, bear right.

Once over a side-crest, another sloping valley awaits you. One last crest is crossed at about **2h30min**. Some 10 minutes later, *keep an eye out for a concrete post above you*, near the top of the ridge; in dusty conditions it's hard to see, but it's about 10 minutes above you at this point. However, if conditions are good, first make for the gravelly HILLOCK below you to the right (**2h50min**), from where you have a fine view out over the beach of Barlovento and the crags of Jandía rearing up just ahead. Then return to the main route and swing up to the CONCRETE POST (**3h10min**), then veer slightly right — towards another gravelly hillock above you to the right.

Hopefully the track should reappear as you near the *cumbre* (you'll see its stone paving through patches of sand). Once over the pass (**Degollada de Mojones; 3h 20min**), join a track coming in from the left (GR131) and descend into the large valley ahead, leaving the wind and flying sand behind. Not far downhill, where the main track heads down right into the *barranco*, keep left (a short-cut), soon rejoining the main track in the stream bed.

About six minutes later, you leave the *barranco* and bear right round the slopes of a hill (**Atalayeja Grande**). More of the valley opens up, and the sea is in sight. Shortly you cross the bed of the wide **Barranco Tras del Lomo** (**3h50min**) that comes down from the right. Minutes later, the track loops back into the **Barranco de Pece-nescal** (SL FV 11). Here you take a short-cut across abandoned fields and rejoin the track on the far side. Looking up the side-valley, a herders' outpost comes into view — the **Casas de Pecenescal**. Loma Negra is the mountain that fills the left side of the valley.

Reaching the main FV2 by the KM 73 MARKER, *it's wise to flag down your bus*. Or, if you want to make this the 'mother of all walks', you can pick up Walk 18: just follow the GR131 down the *barranco* (where there's a bar.)

Walk 16: PICO DE LA ZARZA

Distance: 17km/10.5mi; 5h

Grade: strenuous, with an ascent of 807m/2650ft. The ascent is nearly all on a track, except for the last 25min, where you follow a path to the summit. It can be very hot — or very cold and windy. Not recommended on very windy days — nor on cloudy days, since the climb is only worth it for the view and, if you were lost in mist, the climb could be dangerous as well. But everyone who is fit should try this hike, beginners included.

Equipment: walking boots or stout shoes with ankle support, warm jacket, raingear, sunhat, suncream, picnic, plenty of water

How to get there and return: 🚌 (Lines 01, 04, 05, 09, 10) or 🚗 to/from the Ventura Shopping Center at Jandía Playa, where there is also a large car park (or you could park by the water catchment 10min uphill).

Pico de la Zarza is Fuerteventura's highest peak and worth climbing for two reasons: the grand panorama that tumbles away below you and the wealth of botanical specimens to be seen en route. The best time to scale this mountain is in spring, when the summit is resplendent with yellow-flowering *Asteriscus* (see below). But, be warned: it can be very windy! On a calm day, it's one of the most exhilarating spots on the island.

The walk starts at the BUS STOP in front of the VENTURA SHOPPING CENTER. Follow the FV2 a short way east, to the roundabout with the tall modern sculpture. Turn left here and walk up the wide road beside the Barceló Jandía Playa Hotel. After 300m/yds, turn left on Calle Sancho Panza (there may be a sign here for 'Jandía Golf'). As this road bends round to the right and edges the **Barranco de Vinamar**, aim for a large WATER-

WORKS you can see up ahead. When the road forks, keep right and right again a minute later, to pass to the right of this WATERWORKS and join a track. Nearby is a WALKERS' INFORMATION BOARD for the PR FV 54. Follow the track uphill; it quickly becomes rough and winds its way up the rock- and stone-strewn slopes. Some **12-15min** minutes uphill you cross a track. A stiff climb lies ahead, but you already have a superb view back over the long white Playa del Matorral with its turquoise-green shoreline. The Barranco de Vinamar, as bleak as the rest of the countryside, cuts straight back into the massif.

Climbing higher, you catch sight of corrals hidden in the depths of the ravine. On heading round to the eastern side of the ridge, you overlook another harsh valley (Valluelo de la Cal, with a stone quarry and garbage dump), where more ridges hint at a succession of ravines in the distance. You have an excellent view that stretches to the hills at the centre of the island. Pico de la Zarza is the unimpressive peak that rises a thumbnail above the rest of the massif at the very end of this ridge.

Reaching the cloud zone, you find that the top of the crest is very herbaceous. It's quite a wild garden! (Keep well clear of any goats you may encounter up here; they are very easily frightened and will dart off in all directions if startled; in particular, avoid any with kids.) Climbing higher, you head alongside a bouldery crest, flooded with *tabaiba* bushes, *verode* and asphodels. Look, too, down on the *barranco* walls below, where you'll spot some enormous *candelabra*.

When the track reaches about 500m/1640ft (**2h**) it deteriorates. The track stops dead on the crest of the ridge (**2h35min**), leaving you to continue to the top on a path. *Lamarzkia aurea* (it resembles the bottle-brush plant) flourishes up here, and soon the slopes are ablaze with golden yellow *Asteriscus*. About 200m/yds from the summit, Medio Ambiente has erected a high fence, to

From the summit of Pico de la Zarza, you look out towards the tip of the Jandía Peninsula. There's a surprising amount of greenery up here, including the furry-leafed yellow Asteriscus.

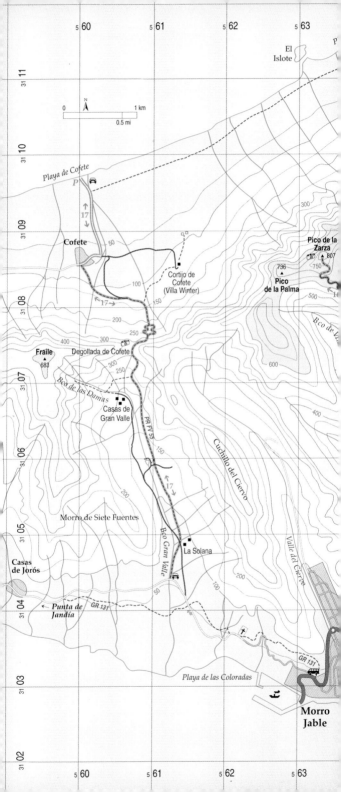

protect the very special flora from goats and sheep. Go through the gate, *making sure to close it behind you.*

Approaching **3h**, windswept and exhausted, you're on the roof of the island, atop **Pico de la Zarza**. And what a view! To the left you look across the lofty crags that rupture this impenetrable wall of rock. The jutting south-western coastline unfolds as this barrier of mountains dies down into sand-patched hills and finally a sea-plain. Don't venture too near to the edge of the peak; it plummets hundreds of feet straight down onto a sea-flat. A mysterious mansion with a turret sits back off the flat, in the shadows of the cliffs — the Cortijo de Cofete (see Walk 17). More in keeping with the landscape is Cofete, the hamlet of small huts over to the left. To your right stand the high rolling sandhills of the Pared isthmus that joins these mountains to the northern half of the island. On hazeless days, it's possible to see well down the eastern coastline to Lanzarote.

Botanists will want to tarry here on the summit for quite some time to discover more of the island's floral treasures: *Echium handiense, Bupleurum handiense, Sideritis massoniana, Argyranthemum winteri,* and the more common *Ranunculus cortusifolius, Andryala cheiran-thifolia* and *Minuartia platyphylla.* The summit also houses a tiny meteorological hut and two large antennae.

Home is all downhill — sheer bliss — two hour's descent away. You'll be back at the FV2 in about **5h**.

Looking from the summit of Pico de la Zarza northeast over Playa de Barlovento (left) and down over the Cortijo de Cofete, to the tail of the Jandía Peninsula (right)

Walk 17: BARRANCO GRAN VALLE • DEGOLLADA DE COFETE • PLAYA DE COFETE • BARRANCO GRAN VALLE

See map pages 96-97   Distance: 15km/9.3mi; 5h

Grade: strenuous, with an overall ascent of 650m/2100ft. The pass (Degollada de Cofete) costs you a 300m/985ft climb — twice. The path on the west coast is rocky and stony. It can be very hot, and there is no shade en route. The beach is usually very windy. But apart from being steep, the walk (PR FV 55) is accessible to everyone.

Equipment: walking boots, warm fleece, sunhat, raingear, suncream, swimwear, picnic, as much water as you can carry

How to get there and return: 🚗 car or taxi to/from the Barranco Gran Valle. Take the road signed for 'Punta de Jandía' on the west side of Morro Jable. After about 3km you pass a water tank on the left, 40m beyond which the GR131 crosses the road. Some 450m further on there is a parking area/information board at the beginning of the PR trail.

Cross the Jandía Peninsula to the isolated west coast and see what isolated really means! From the crest of the *cumbre* you will have magnificent sweeping views along the beaches of Cofete and Barlovento de Jandía. The empty beaches and crashing breakers are enough to send anyone running down to meet them. Make sure you're fit enough to tackle this hike, however!

The walk begins 500 m past a WATER TANK on the gravel road, 3km west of Morro Jable, where a clear path begins by an INFORMATION BOARD for the PR FV 55. From here head straight into the ravine. Standing at the entrance to this austere *barranco,* you can see all the way to the end of it. An abandoned settlement of stone corrals sits at the foot of the lofty summits. On either side of you the valley floor sweeps back up into severe rocky walls. Out here you meet only goats and sheep. Keep an eye out for the rare cactus-like *Euphorbia handiensis* (Jandía cactus spurge) on this walk (see photograph page 26). It only grows in a few places south of Morro Jable. The only other vegetation in this stony terrain is the tobacco plant, *cosco, Lycium intricatum,* and *aulaga.*

A little over **5min** along, you reach the two large CORRALS of **La Solana**, with pens constructed out of everything from fishing nets to metal. You cross a track* and continue on a well-defined, manicured footpath, passing above an EARTHEN-WALLED DAM (**15min**). Further into the valley you're looking out onto the tired stone pens of **Casas de Gran Valle**, the old pastoral outpost you could see from the start of the walk. In the past this area was an aboriginal settlement; some of

*This leads to Casas de Gran Valle, from where you could rejoin the path to the pass.

their small stone dwellings are still clearly visible. You cross a couple of dry side-streams before the real ascent begins.

At the foot of the pass the way swings back to the right to begin a zigzag ascent. In the past, this was the main route across the peninsula; it has now been restored. A grassy plant, *Lamarzkia aurea*, flanks the path. Nearing the col, you cross a colourful bare rock-face.

Keeping to the right-hand side of the pass, you cross the **Degollada de Cofete (1h20min)** and look up at towering crags that stand like sentries on either side. The sharp, pointed peak on the left is called Fraile. Stretching out below you are the striking golden beaches of Cofete (left) and Barlovento de Jandía (right). A chateau-like villa with a turret (so bizarrely-sited in this bleak landscape) immediately captures your attention. Stories abound about this amazing house, and it still remains shrouded in mystery. It belonged to a Sr Winter, a German engineer who came to the island before World War II and eventually owned the entire peninsula. When the house was built in the early 1940s, he forbade his workers (or anyone, for that matter) to live in Cofete. Everyone had to return to Morro Jable at the end of the day. And from then on, stories have grown about the place — which would have been a good setting for a Hitchcock film! Cofete is the outpost of stone and cement-block huts nearby, its ugliness eclipsed by the dazzling stretch of coastline.

Below the pass the good clear path, sometimes hewn from the rock, continues down to the right. The lichen-flecked pinnacles of rock that pierce this range keep

Top: view from the Degollada de Cofete down over the mysterious Villa Winter. Bottom: a colony of Euphorbias *near Cofete*

drawing your attention. This chain of volcanic mountains harbours the island's most interesting flora. Behind you, the *riscos* (cliffs) rise up into dark sinister shadows.

Accompanied by large, but friendly, yellow grasshoppers desporting themselves in the *Gramineae*, some 45 minutes below the pass you come to a crossing track (**2h10min**). Here you follow the path towards the houses and huts of Cofete. Wine-red *cosco* (and the fort-like bar/restaurant a short way downhill) provide

the only colour in this sun-bleached countryside. From Cofete head east along a track*; keep left at a fork, then head straight down to the **Playa de Cofete** (**2h30min**). Expect company from about 11am onwards; this side of the peninsula has been 'discovered', but there's still plenty of beach for everyone. The undertow here is treacherous, and swimming would be foolhardy!

Home is back the way you came, over the pass, and you're back at the CAR PARK in **5h**.

---

*This track leads to Villa Winter. Go on! You know you want to see it up close! On my last visit the house was inhabited by an elderly couple, and most of the building could be visited. The bar in Cofete was built by the same company as the villa — notice the similarity of the walls.

WALK 18: FROM MORRO JABLE TO COSTA CALMA ALONG THE BEACH

See also map pages 88-89   **Distance:** 14km/8.7mi; 4h

Grade: easy, but walking continuously on sand is fairly tiring. Don't attempt on a windy day, when it could be very unpleasant.

Equipment: sandals, sunhat, suncream, sunglasses, long sleeved shirt, swimwear, picnic, plenty of water

How to get there: 🚌 to Club Aldiana (Lines 01, 04, 05, 09, 10)
To return: 🚌 from the turn-off to the Hotel Gorriones, south of Costa Calma on the FV2 (Lines 01, 04, 05, 09, 10; map pages 88-89)

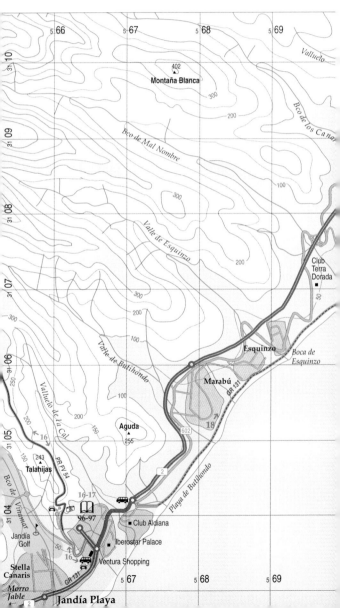

Beach, beer, and bare bods: that's what this walk is all about. This is the stretch of coastline that has made Fuerteventura famous. Take the bare minimum with you; a number of small bars en route make perfect refueling stations. If you're expecting solitude, forget it — but there's plenty of space for everyone on Playa de Sotovento de Jandía. Make a day of it.

The walks starts at **Club Aldiana**. Take the road on the north side of the complex and make your way down to the beach, and you're away — passing the first bar immediately. Since everybody either builds their own stone wind shelters here, or adds to the ones they've bought, this beach looks like an archeological site of old Guanche ruins. And did I mention: clothes *off* is the rule rather than the exception on this stretch of coastline.

When this beach ends, you clamber over stones to continue along the next one — a large bay with buildings

103

on both sides of the mouth of
the **Barranco de Butihondo**.
This is an umbrella and
sunbed beach, with several
bars thrown in. Crossing
stones and rounding a sandhill, you're into your third
beach. Mass tourism is behind
you now. This beach is
another fortification of stone-
built shelters. Flags hoisted
means occupied: find your
own wind-shelter!

The further north you go,
the more beautiful the
beaches. Leaving the bay
behind, you cross a stretch of
rocks, and look up into a
barranco free of buildings. Around the corner lies another
equally beautiful beach, with just a few sunbeds and
brollies. At the back of it there's a SIGN for **Club Tierra
Dorada (1h30min)**, which sits on the hillside above.
Towards the end of the beach you can quench your thirst
at another bar. On clear days the island's midriff, the hilly
interior, can be seen curving around to the right from
here, and a collar of sand leads the eye along to another
beach.

Two long arms of dunes run down to the next beach,
at the mouth of the **Barranco de Pescenescal** (where
Walk 15 ends). El Paso (253m) is the hill ahead that
outsizes all the others. A small corner of houses at the end
of the *playa* (the **Casas Risco del Paso**) is the only damage
done here, and there is another beach bar.

Past these houses, you come upon the jewel — **Playa
de Sotavento de Jandía (2h10min)**: it's on the cover of
every tourist brochure. Ahead is a sweeping sand bar with
tidal lagoons. When the tide is out, this sandy promontory
extends several hundred metres out from the shore, and
you can make your way along it (otherwise, just follow
the shore). A small beach bar appears below a rocky
protrusion. The Hotel Gorriones is the eyesore on this
stretch of coastline — at least it calls your attention to the
nearest bus stop. In the distance to the left, a few of the
nearby wind generators come into sight. The shoreline sea

is a beryl green; beyond that it's deep blue. At **3h30min** you're level with the hotel.

If you're ready to call it a day here, then go no further. Walk over to the **Hotel Gorriones** (**3h40min**). If you're heading towards Costa Calma, you can catch a bus from behind the hotel (but note, not all buses call in here). If you're heading south towards Morro Jable, you have to catch the bus on the main FV2, which is another 20 minutes uphill past the hotel (**4h**).

If you're still enjoying the walk, turn to the map on pages 88-89. The Costa Calma beach lies another hour away, and the nearest bus stop 25 minutes beyond it. Just keep on along the sand bar, then follow the coast. Three more pretty coves, full of naked souls, lie on route. If the tide is high, take the track above the sea, then descend to the main beach. At Costa Calma, those catching a bus for the north will find their stop behind the **Fuerteventura Playa Hotel**, at the end of the beach. If you're south-bound, take the road from the Fuerteventura Playa Hotel up to the FV2. Cross this main road and at the next roundabout, find the BUS STOP just opposite — off to the right.

Lanzarote

Touring map*   *reverse of Fuerteventura touring map*

*The numbers on this touring map indicate car tours and walks in the
book *Landscapes of Lanzarote*.

Car tour 4: A DAY OUT ON LANZAROTE

Playa Blanca • El Golfo • Yaiza • Parque Nacional de Timanfaya • Tinajo • La Santa • Monumento al Campesino • La Geria • Uga • Femés • Playa Blanca

95km/59mi; 4 hours driving (plus 25-40 minutes on the ferry each way and any driving on Fuerteventura to reach Corralejo)

On route: Walks 19-22

*This is a **very** long day. **Do** plan on taking the first ferry in the morning and returning on the last one. There is no need to pre-book (outside the major holidays); just turn up about half an hour before sailing time and buy your tickets at the office on the pier in Corralejo. This tour takes in the south of Lanzarote — it's just not practicable to get to the north on a day trip from Fuerteventura, especially since you should allow at least an hour for your bus tour of the Timanfaya National Park and another half hour for the Visitors' Centre. To visit the famous Famara cliffs or Jameos del Agua in the north, you should spend at least one night on the island. Petrol stations are plentiful and roads are good, but be careful, some roads drop off sharply at the sides, into the vineyards or lava below — take special care here, as the scenery is so eye-catching that you could easily drive off the road. See map of Lanzarote on the reverse of the Fuerteventura touring map inside the back cover, and plan of Playa Blanca on pages 114-115.*

This route is short, but action-packed. You'll use up a whole day trying to fit everything in. And throughout the tour you'll be amazed at how the short ferry journey has taken you to a completely different world!

Referring to the plan on pages 114-115, head away

from the port at Playa Blanca and turn right on the main road. At the roundabout (where the bus station, 'Estación de Guaguas' is to the left), turn left up to the next roundabout (). Take the *third* exit from the roundabout, the LZ701 signposted for Yaiza. This old road runs parallel with the newer LZ2 'raceway' over to the right, zipping straight across the flat and featureless Rubicón Plain. Montaña Atalaya captures your attention on the right: on the way home you'll ascend high into its hidden valleys. The small village of Las Breñas, set back on a shelf off the plain, sits at the foot of Atalaya. Some 7km along, notice the isolated dark yellow building on the left; Walk 20 starts at this water desalination plant. The next eye-catcher is the salt pans, the **Salinas de Janubio★** (⌾), on the left. This basin of tiny rectangles reflects many tones of red, pink and orange in the intense sunlight.

Just beyond the salt pans, at 9.5km, you turn off for El Golfo. (Roundabout fever has caught on in Lanzarote, too.) Pass through **La Hoya** (⌾✕), a few houses set back off the salt pans. Circling behind the pans, you get a clear view straight across them. A lagoon separates the salt pans from the black-sand beach of Playa de Janubio. Suddenly you're swallowed up in *malpais* ('badland') lava. Superb

sea views follow as you drive parallel with the coast. Several roadside parking bays allow you to pull over to enjoy the views (📷) of the low jagged and jutting lava sea-cliffs. Then you come to the most famous outlook on this stretch of road, **Los Hervideros★** (📷; the 'boiling springs'), with a very large parking area. Here walkways have been carefully laid out through the maze of lava, where the waves pound into sea-caves and you might get a soaking from some impressive blow-holes. Montaña Bermeja breaks the monochrome landscape with its rusty-red slopes.

Less than 2km further on, take the signposted turn-off left to the **Charco de Los Clicos★**, a cloudy green lagoon at the base of the El Golfo crater (photograph page 112). Then return to the main road and continue towards El Golfo. Circling behind the crater, turn left when you come to a junction. As the road descends, you'll see a parking area on the left *(not signposted)*, full of vehicles. This *mirador* affords an excellent view (📷) over the eroded **Golfo crater★**. This majestic, mostly-submarine volcano has been spectacularly eaten away by the sea, leaving one with the impression that it has been sliced in half. A path used to descend from here to the Charco de los Clicos, but it has been closed off to prevent erosion. From the viewpoint carry on down to the small seaside village of **El Golfo** (17km ✕), bustling with fish restaurants.

Return to the junction near the viewpoint and go left for Yaiza. Heading inland, volcanic mounds begin appearing. As you drive between two prominent cone-shaped hills, the ubiquitous Montaña Atalaya reappears. Passing under the LZ2, you join a roundabout, circle it and follow the *very small sign* indicating Yaiza. The road is lined with palms, aloes, and *tabaiba*. **Yaiza** (26km ✝✕⛽⊕) is neat, charming and spotless — manicured, in fact! The dark stone walls and *lapilli* fields make the white houses stand out even more. You pass the Iglesia de Los Remedios that stands in a square of the same name (photograph page 112).

Just past the church, turn left for the Montañas del Fuego. A junction follows: keep straight ahead through it. Passing under the LZ2 again, come to roundabout and go straight over. Soon you enter the **Parque Nacional de Timanfaya★** — announced by the symbol of the devil on the park's sign! Once again you're swallowed up by *mal-pais. (Note: you're not allowed to venture off the road while driving through the park.)* The island's showpiece, Pico

Timanfaya, appears on the left. Both the mountain and the park take their name from the village of Timanfaya, which thrived in this rich agricultural area before being destroyed by six years of eruptions, beginning in 1730. The lichen-flecked lava gives the impression of sleet. It's an array of rich reds, browns, and charcoal. Further along more mounds ooze rust-brown. The turbulent landscape gives the impression you're experiencing the aftermath of a *recent* eruption.

If you fancy a ride on a camel, this is your chance, as you'll pass the **camel station**★ on your left, 9km out of Yaiza. Even just watching the camel trains can be fun. Descending into a basin, you come to the park entrance

Los Hervideros, with the rust-red slopes of Montaña Bermeja in the background

Charco de los Clicos (top), church and square of Los Remedio in Yaiza (middle), and the half-moon stone walls protecting young vines in the lapilli *fields of La Geria (bottom)*

(34.5km) and turn off left for the **Islote de Hilario** — departure point for the coach tours around the **Montañas del Fuego★**. An entrance fee, which includes the tour, is paid here. After the park, your next stop should be the **Centro de Visitantes** (38.5km), with its excellent audio-visual show and exhibits. Farmlands follow, with fields of potatoes, onions, grapes, and low bushy fig trees.

Just outside the park boundary, **Mancha Blanca** (39.5km) sits on a crest overlooking the fields. Leaving the village, you come to a junction and bear left for Tinajo/La Santa. **Tinajo** (41km ♦✕🍽) is an affluent farming town. Note the balconied Canarian homes. The town stretches out for some 3km: as you drive through it, keep right when the way forks. Heading straight over a roundabout, you cross an open barren plain. On this stretch of road, you'll encounter many cyclists in training from the La Santa sports complex. First you pass through the village of **La Santa** (47km ✕) and, 2km further on, you come to Club La Santa, a rather exclusive sports complex. It overlooks the rocky islet, La Isleta, and a pretty lagoon where all the wind-surfing takes place. To cross the *isleta*, curve left past the hotel reception and, when you come to a roundabout, keep right. Circle halfway round the islet; then, keeping the lagoon just to your left, cross the causeway and return to the main road.

Drive back to Tinajo and keep left on the LZ20 for

San Bartolomé/Arrecife. **Tiagua** (61.5km ✕M), a typical farming village follows. In **Tao** (63km ✕📷) you experience a change in landscape. Grassy inclines begin appearing. Palms grace the village, which spreads over hillsides and hollows (photograph overleaf). Descending, you come into yet another small village, **Mozaga** (66km ✕🍽). Its fame rests on César Manrique's **Monumento al Campesino★** at the large roundabout — make of it what you will.

Circling this roundabout, bear right on the LZ30 for **La Geria★**, the 'wine valley'. Aside from tourism, this is the most

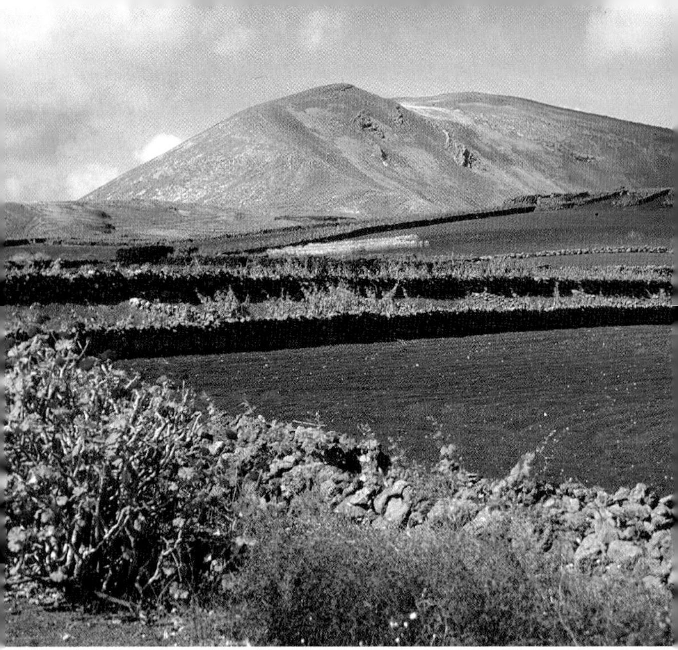

prosperous enterprise on the island. **Masdache** (68km ✕) is a well-dispersed village. From here on you'll pass several well-known *bodegas.* La Geria occupies a basin off the lava flow. The landscape here, pitted with hollows, is intriguing. The slopes are coated in black ash, and a myriad of low half-moon stone walls *(zocos)* edge the hollows and

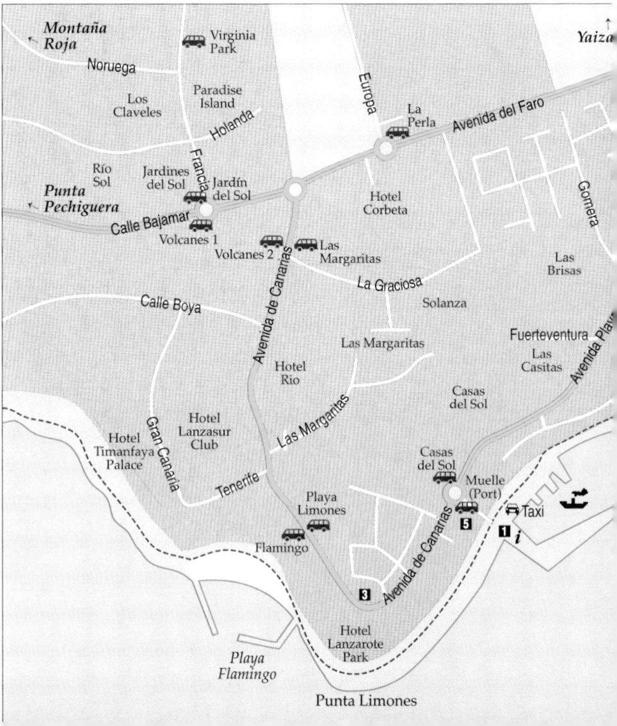

Pastoral landscape near Tao

stretch across the countryside. This is the home of *malvasia* wine, the product of an ingenious farming method: the vines are planted in crater-like depressions layered with *lapilli,* which absorb moisture from the air and enable a single vine to produce as much as 200 kilos of grapes annually.

Crossing a crest, you descend to a junction (83.5km), with Montaña Atalaya staring straight at you. It overshadows **Uga** (✕), a sprawling village immediately over to your right. The LZ30 ends at a round-about: go straight over, crossing the the LZ2, to begin the ascent to Femés (LZ702). This landscape, with its grassy hillsides, is more akin to the north of Lanzarote. Looking back, tremendous views of the inland hills unravel. Passing through the small village of **Las Casitas de Femés**, you ascend into a larger valley. Fields lie on either side of the road. **Femés** (88km ✕🛏; Walk 22; photographs page 125) sits around the upper slopes of Montaña Atalaya. From the *mirador* in front of the church, the Balcón de Femés, you have a fine view over the Rubicón Plain to Playa Blanca, framed by the hills.

At the roundabout below Femés, keep left for Playa Blanca, driving across the plain and straight over roundabouts. You come back to the roundabout by the bus station in **Playa Blanca**, from where the port is straight ahead.

If you're running earlier than expected, all the recommended leg-stretchers are close by: the two climbs from Femés (Walk 22), Walk 20 from the desalination plant, and a choice of two from Playa Blanca itself (Walks 19 and 21).

Walk 19: MONTAÑA ROJA

See also town plan pages 8-9   **Distance:** 3km/2mi; 1h05min

Grade: an easy climb/descent of 130m/425ft, but the volcanic pumice underfoot is slippery. An ideal walk for those with children. No shade.

Equipment: comfortable walking shoes with ankle support, fleece, sunhat, suncream, water

How to get there and return: 🚗 to the roundabout outside Playa Blanca, then take the road for 'Faro de Pechiguera'. Pass the Corbeta Hotel on the left after about 1km, go straight over the next roundabout and, at the next (third) roundabout, turn right for Jardines del Sol (among others). Pass Los Claveles on the left, then keep ahead following the sign 'To the Volcano'. Park around here in one of the streets below the easily-seen path up the crater. Or: town 🚌 30 to Virginia Park. Sometimes the names are missing from the bus stops: Virginia Park is the second stop after Colegio. From the stop walk seaward, then take the first right (Calle de Noruega), passing Los Claveles on the left.

Montaña Roja is just a little pimple of a volcano, but in spring wonderful miniature gardens of wild flowers flourish in the pumice and, as the mountain rises in isolation on the Rubicón plain, it affords far-reaching views. At the end of your day out on Lanzarote, if you still have time before the last ferry, this short leg-stretcher will give you Lanzarote's finest views across to Fuerteventura and the sand dues of Corralejo.

Start out at the 'TO THE VOLCANO' sign: follow the street uphill to access the path. It's only **15min** up to the rim, where you can go either left or right. (Turn left if

you're in a hurry, and you'll reach the trig point in only 10 minutes.) The main walk heads right, passing a path into the bottom of the crater, just 20m below. The crater floor is disfigured with 'graffiti' — small stones arranged to spell out the names of previous visitors. As you round the basin, the urban sprawl and a network of roads comes into view — one leading to the large Atlante del Sol ruin in the northwest, an urbanization that was never completed. It stands isolated in a desert wilderness.

In about **45min** or a little more you will reach the **Montaña Roja** TRIG POINT, the highest point of the walk (194m). From here there's a fine view down to the lighthouses at Pechiguera and over to the dunes of Corralejo.

You'll be back at the junction in another 10 minutes and down at the 'VOLCANO' SIGN in **1h 05min**.

Rounding the small crater of Montaña Roja, you look down to the lighthouses at the Punta de Pechiguera. In the immediate surroundings are 'rock gardens', where delicate wild flowers flourish amidst white- and orange-crust lichens (top) and leaf-lichen (middle).

LANZAROTE

Playa de Janubio

6 10 6 11 6 12 6 13

32 00

31 99

20

20

31 98

25

Piedra Alta

El Convento

31 97

Costa de Rubicón

20

Punta Gorda

Atlante del Sol

31 96

50

701
2

31 95

100

Montaña Roja

19

Colegio

Virginia Park

150

Faro Park

194

150

Mña Baja

Los Claveles

Paradise Island

50

Río Sol

Jardines del Sol

Castillo

Corbeta

50

Pla Bla

Playa Montaña Roja

Playa Blanca

Faro de Pechiguera
Punta de Pechiguera

Punta Limones

31 92

0   N   1 km

0.5 mi

Corral

31 91

6 10 6 11 6 12 6 13 6 14

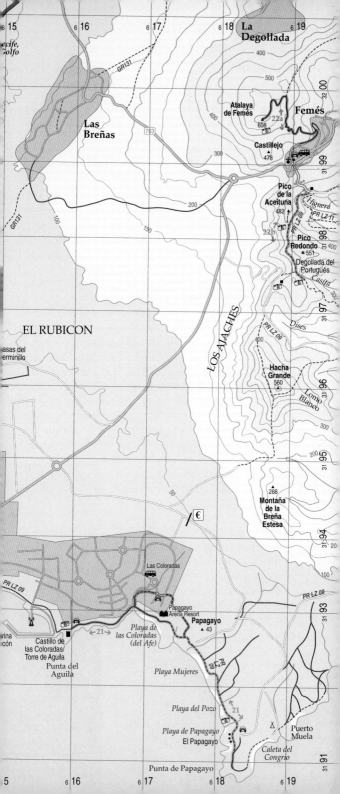

Walk 20: THE ROCK POOLS OF JANUBIO

Map pages 118-119   Distance: 6km/3.7mi; 2h

Grade: moderate; the terrain is mostly level underfoot, but you're floundering over uneven lava for much of the way. The final descent to El Convento is vertiginous and dangerous if wet (but this may be omitted).

Equipment: stout shoes with grip or walking boots, sunhat, suncream, fleece, raingear, picnic, plenty of water, swimwear

How to get there and return: 🚌 to/from the water desalination plant — a large isolated dark yellow building off the FV701 (old road), 2.4km south of the El Golfo roundabout. Ample parking.

This coastal walk, with its superb unvisited rock pools, is an ideal leg-stretcher on a hot day. You follow a jagged, rocky coastline. There are no beaches, only natural rock pools — pools to suit all the family — hidden on the lava shelves that jut out into the sea. El Convento is an impressive sea cave you can visit en route.

Start the walk at the WATER DESALINATION PLANT: go down to the lava rocks near the shore and head left (southwest). About 10-15 minutes beyond the desalination plant you begin finding the best pools, so keep an eye out for them. The sea churns up against the shelf, replenishing these pools: obviously, swimming isn't recommended in bad weather or when the sea is rough. At **10min**, from the edge of the plain, you'll spot a first seashelf with a number of pools embedded in it. A few minutes' scrambling over rocks and boulders brings you down to them. This is an excellent spot for children, but the pools are also deep enough for adults. Some eight minutes later, there is another vast shelf with more inviting pools. Finally, a few minutes past this spot, you will find a magnificent solitary pool. All of these emerald-green waterholes are simply irresistible…

Attention is needed at about **1h 10min**: shortly after turning inland (behind a small 'dip') to avoid a mass of lava rock, you pass a round white CONCRETE TRIG MARKER (**Piedra Alta**) that stands on a point to your right. Here you scramble over all the rock, to the top of the cliffs, for a dramatic coastal overlook. Two inviting green pools lie in what

The rock pools near the water desalination plant are frequented by fishermen.

120

appears to be an inaccessible shelf, immediately below. Behind the pools stands an enormous cave — **El Convento** — with a 'cloistered' entrance opening back into the face of the cliff. A smaller cave sits to its right. Now the problem is: how to get there?

The safest way down is just beyond the second cave, some four to five minutes round the top of the cliff. You cross some interesting rock formations, resembling large fragments of broken crockery. Straight off this area of rock, you drop down onto 'lumps' of lava. Metres to the right (close to the edge of the cliff), a nose of rock reveals itself. Make sure that breakers aren't crashing over the shelf, and then descend *with care* to this superb and sheltered spot. All fours are needed, and this descent is only recommended for very sure-footed walkers. When the sea is calm, there is no danger.

A blow hole lies a further 20 minutes along the coast, if you have the time. It's more noticeable for its noise than the spray of water. You'll find it on a sea-shelf set in the U of the next bay along. The noise gives it away.

The return is much easier on the feet: you follow a track that lies just a few minutes back from the top of the cliff — slightly inland from the path. Heading back, you have a good view of the Golfo crater — the prominent orange-coloured cone rising up off the seashore. Remain on the track along the coast; ignore all turn-offs inland. By **2h** you should be back at the DESALINATION PLANT.

Walk 21: CASTILLO DE LAS COLORADAS • PUNTA DE PAPAGAYO • CASTILLO DE LAS COLORADAS

Map pages 118-119   **Distance:** 9km/5.6mi; 2h50min

Grade: easy, but there is no shade en route, and it can be very hot.

Equipment: comfortable walking shoes, fleece, sunhat, suncream, raingear, picnic, water, swimwear

How to get there and return: 🚌 to/from the Castillo de las Coloradas, just east of Playa Blanca. (Or shorten the walk to 6km/3.7mi; 1h55min by driving *past* the Castillo de las Coloradas and parking near the Papagayo Arena Resort Hotel.)

If you would like to see 'how the other half lives', then head out to Punta de Papagayo and *Lanzarote's* finest beaches. After Sotavento de Jandía you are sure to be underwhelmed — but then Lanzarote is all about volcanoes, not *playas*…

Start off at the well-restored **Castillo de las Coloradas** (1769; also called **Torre de Aguila**). Off this headland you have a good view towards the beaches scooped out of the open bay on your left which culminates in the Punta de Papagayo. Head east on the wide brick-paved COASTAL PROMENADE; it rises and falls as it curves along the coast past several large apartment and hotel complexes. After crossing a BRIDGE, you come to **Playa de las Coloradas** (also called **Playa del Afe**); this stony beach is the ugly duckling of these *playas*. Just past the beach the promenade ends in front of the HOTEL PAPAGAYO ARENA, from where a steep and skiddy path leads up to the headland.*
Once at the top, you find a clear path over to Playa Mujeres. Low spiny *aulaga* lies scattered across the plain.

Some **35min** into the walk the unspoilt **Playa Mujeres** is in sight. This lovely open beach stretches across the mouth of a shallow *barranco*. El Papagayo, the only sign of civilisation out here, is the handful of buildings near the point. Your path drops down into a small gravelly *barranco* and mounts a faint track which leads you down onto the golden sandy beach. Behind you are the windswept hills of Los Ajaches. Near the end of the beach, scale the sandy bank to remount the crest — a steep, three-minute climb on sand and loose gravel. Continuing along the top of the crest, you dip in and out of small *barrancos* which empty out into concealed coves below.

*This path is the 'traditional' route: everybody uses it. But if you don't fancy the scramble, walk back 400m/yds and turn right just before the bridge, heading for the signposted commercial centre. Pass a parking area and, 150m/yds from the seafront, bear right. Pick up a path between the commercial centre to the right and gardens to the left. A blue walkers' sign indicates 'Playas de Papagayo' from here. In a couple of minutes an information board signals the the new 'official' trail to the headland.

Playa del Pozo is the next of the larger beaches. You can either clamber down a narrow stream bed to reach it, or follow the trail straight on down the ridge (easier). Ascending the goats' path that edges the hillside at the end of the beach, once again you're above the sea. (If this path strikes you as vertiginous, just scramble straight up from the beach to the plain.) Now more enticing coves reveal themselves. Soon the old settlement of Papagayo reappears on the crest of the ridge ahead. Circling behind a couple of coves, you reach the top of the crest and come to **El Papagayo (1h15min)**; there are three bar/restaurants here, if you're in need of refreshment. A rust-brown and deep mauve-coloured rocky promontory separates the two dazzling coves on either side of you. From here you have a striking view of the smooth-faced inland hills, as well as along the string of beaches you've just visited.

Continue on the path curving round Playa de Papagayo. Below you is the beach and some tents fastened to the face of the hill. (If you find this path unnerving, just walk along the top of the crest.) Soon meeting a track coming in from the left, follow it out to **Punta de Papagayo (1h25min)**. Don't go too near the edge of the cliffs on windy days! From here Fuerteventura is very close, and Lobos stands out against the dunes of Corralejo.

Return the same way to the **Castillo de las Coloradas/ Torre de Aguila (2h50min)**.

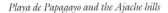
Playa de Papagayo and the Ajache hills

Walk 22: AROUND FEMÉS

Map pages 118-119   **Distance, grade:** as individual walks below
Equipment: stout shoes with good ankle support (or walking boots), warm jacket, sunhat, raingear, suncream, picnic, water
How to get there and return: 🚌 to/from Femés

Walk a: Femés — Atalaya de Femés — Femés (3.2km/2mi; 1h30min). A strenuous, but short, ascent/descent of 300m/1000ft.

Walk b: Femés — Degollada del Portugués — Femés (3.5km/2.2mi; 1h35min). Climb and descent of only 100m/330ft, but there is a possibility of vertigo on one stretch.

Both of these short walks afford tremendous views. If you have the energy, the view from the Atalaya de Femés (Walk a) is unquestionably the finer, as it affords views over both Timanfaya and the Salinas de Janubio.

Start Walk a facing the **Bar Femés** on the main road: walk up the road at its left-hand side, keeping the church on your left. You will meet a brick-paved road: follow it uphill to the right. At the top of the road, where it bends right to rejoin the main road, take the concrete track up to the left (just in front of a green garage door). This track takes you all the way to the access track to the transmitter station). At the **Atalaya de Femés** (608m/ 1995ft; **50min**) a stupendous view unfolds. The remote (for this island!) little village of Femés lies straight below, huddled around the pass that descends to the Rubicón Plain. Fuerteventura and Lobos fill in the backdrop. And from up here you can almost count the colourful volcanoes of Timanfaya. Return the same way to the BAR (**1h30min**).

Start Walk b at the ROUNDABOUT on the main road in **Femés** by following the PR LZ 09 finger-posts up the tarred lane opposite the Bar Femés, making for some ugly concrete buildings seen ahead on the hilltop. The tarmac peters out, and you pass between two *aljibes* (water tanks set into the ground). Walk just to the right of the main building, still on the road/track. Looking to the left now, the reason for this blot on the landscape reveals itself: there's the amusing sight of a GOAT FARM, and the large pen may be bursting with these delightful creatures. The buildings lie at the edge of a crest, overlooking the uninhabited **Higuera Valley** (**10min**) — a huge abyss where, straight below you, the dry river bed traces an intricate meander in a pristine landscape. Your ongoing path, the sign-posted PR LZ 09, is to your right, accompanied by a black pipe. Walk towards it, passing

to the left of another building half sunken into the rock, and bearing slightly left downhill. Crossing a saddle between **Pico de la Aceituna** and **Pico Redondo** (**30min**), you enjoy a fine view over the Rubicón Plain. By **40min** a new *barranco* drops away steeply to the right. Some people may find this stretch unnerving, but the path is amply wide. Five minutes later, go left at a fork, climbing the flanks of Pico Redondo to the **Degollada del Portugués** (**47min**). Retrace your steps to **Femés** (**1h35min**).

View over Femés on the ascent to the Atalaya de Femés (top); Femés church (middle); the Rubicón Plain and Playa Blanca from the ascent to the Degollada

BUS AND FERRY TIMETABLES

BUSES

The operator is Tiadhe: tel (34) 928 852166; www.tiadhe.com. There are more services than those shown here. Be sure to pick up a current timetable when you arrive or check the web.

Line 01: Pto Rosario — Morro Jable (via Antigua, Gran Tarajal, Tarajalejo and Costa Calma); journey time approximately 2h15min
Departs Pto Rosario (Mon-Fri) 06.30-22.30, hourly on the half hour (except 18.30); *(Sat)* 07.00, then 08.30-14.30 hourly on the half hour, 16.00. 1900, 21.30; *(Sun, holidays)* 09.00, 11.00, 12.15, 13.30, 14.30, 17.00, 19.00, 20.30. *Departs Morro Jable (Mon-Fri)* 06.00, 8.00-14.00 hourly on the hour,15.30, 16.30, 17.30, 19.00, 20.00, 22.30; *(Sat)* 07.00, 08.00, 09.30, 11.00, 12.30, 14.00, 15.30, 16.30, 19.00, 22.30; *(Sun, holidays)* 08.00, 09.30, 11.30, 14.00, 15.30, 16.45, 19.00, 22.30

Line 02: Puerto del Rosario — Vega de Río Palmas (via the Tefía junction, Llanos de la Concepción and Betancuria); journey time approximately 1h30min
Departs Pto Rosario (daily) 11.00, 14.30; *Departs Vega de Río Palmas (daily)* 12.30, 16.30

Line 03: Puerto del Rosario — Caleta de Fuste; journey time approximately 25min
Departs Pto Rosario (Mon-Sat) 06.30-22.00 every half hour; *(Sun)* 07.00-22.00 every hour. *Departs Caleta de Fuste (Mon-Sat)* 07.00-22.00 every half hour; *(Sun)* 07.30-22.30 every hour.

Line 04: Pájara — Morro Jable (via Ajuy, Tuineje, Gran Tarajal and the coastal resorts); journey time approximately 2h15min
Departs Pájara daily at 06.30. *Departs Morro Jable daily* at 16.15

Line 05: Morro Jable — Costa Calma; journey time approximately 35min
Departs Morro Jable (Mon-Sat) 08.30, 09.30, 10.30, 11.30, 12.30, 13.30, 14.30; *(Sun, holidays)* 09.30, 10.30, 11.30, 12.30, 13.30. *Departs Costa Calma (Mon-Sat)* 9.30, 10.30, 11.30, 12.30, 13.15 14.30, 15.30; *(Sun, holidays)* 10.30, 11.30, 12.30, 13.30, 14.30

Line 06: Puerto del Rosario — Corralejo; journey time approximately 50min
Departs Puerto del Rosario (Mon-Sat) 07.00-18.30 every half hour (*except* 13.30, 15.00), then 19.00, 20.00, 21.00, 22.00, 23.00; *(Sun, holidays)* 07.00-21.00 hourly, except 15.00. *Departs Corralejo (Mon-Sat)* 07.00-19.00 every half hour (except 13.30, 15.00), then 20.00, 21.00, 22.00; *(Sun, holidays)* 07.00-21.00 hourly, except 15.00

Line 07: Puerto del Rosario — El Cotillo (via Tindaya, La Oliva, Corralejo and Lajares); journey time approximately 2h
Departs Pto Rosario daily 10.00, 14.15, 19.00. *Departs El Cotillo daily* 06.30, 12.00, 17.00

Line 08: Corralejo — El Cotillo (via Lajares and La Oliva); journey time about 50min
Departs Corralejo daily 09.00-21.00 every hour on the hour. *Departs El Cotillo daily* 8.00-20.00 every hour on the hour except for 14.00

Line 09: Pájara — Morro Jable (via La Pared and Costa Calma); journey time approximately 2h15min
Departs Pájara daily 06.30. *Departs Morro Jable daily* 16.00.

Line 10 Pto Rosario — Morro Jable (via the airport, Caleta de Fuste, Las Salinas, Gran Tarajal and Costa Calma); journey time approximately 2h
Departs Pto Rosario (Mon-Sat) 9.00, 13.45, 16.00 (not Sat), 18.00; *(Sun)* 13.00, 18.00. *Departs Morro Jable (Mon-Sat)* 6.30, 11.30, 13.30 (not Sat), 15.45; *(Sun)* 09.00, 16.00

FERRIES TO/FROM LOBOS (see www.islalobos.es)

'Isla de Los Lobos'; **daily;** *departs Corralejo* 10.00; *last return* 16.00 (18.00 in summer)
'El Majorero'; **daily;** *departs Corralejo* 10.00, 12.00; *returns* 12.30, 16.00
'Celia Cruz'; **daily;** *departs Corralejo* 09.45; *returns* 14.20 or 17.00

FERRIES TO/FROM LANZAROTE

'Bocayna Express' (Fred Olsen Line; www.fredolsen.es) from Corralejo to Playa Blanca; journey time 25min
Departs Corralejo daily 09.00, 12.00, 15.00, 17.00, 19.00 (Mon and Fri only); also 06.30, 07.45 Mon-Fri. *Departs Playa Blanca daily* 08.30, 10.00, 14.00, 16.00, 18.00, 20.00 (Mon and Fri only); also 07.10 Mon-Fri

'Volcan de Tindaya' (Armas Line; www.naviera-armas.com) from Corralejo to Playa Blanca; journey time 40min
Departs Corralejo daily 08.00, 10.00, 12.00 (*not Sun*), 14.00, 18.00, 20.00
Departs Playa Blanca daily 07.00, 09.00, 11.00, 13.15 (*not Sun*), 15.00, 17.00, 19.00

✺ Index

Geographical names comprise the only entries in this Index; for other entries, see Contents, page 3. **Bold-face type** indicates a photograph; *italic type* indicates a map. Both may be in addition to a text reference on the same page.